THE PROHIBITION OF *RIBĀ* ELABORATED

Imran Ahsan Khan Nyazee

Center for Excellence in Research
Islamabad

Center for Excellence in Research,
Head Office: No. 103, Street 2, PTV Colony,
Shahpur, Islamabad,
Pakistan 44000

First Published: 2009
Second Edition: 2016

CENTER FOR EXCELLENCE IN RESEARCH

Dedicated to

Shams ul-A'immah Abū Bakr Muḥammad ibn Aḥmad Abī Sahl al-Sarakhsī
(d. 483 A.H.)

وانا انبهك – ايّها المسترشد – على شاكلة الصواب، قبل ان اخوض بك في غمرة الكتاب، واقدم اليك نصيحة مشوبة بخشونة؛ فلا يزوينّك عنها مرارة مذاقها، وخشونة ملمسها فنصيحة في تخشين خير من خديعة في لين: وهي: أن هذا الكتاب لن يسمح بمضمون اسراره على مطالع، ولن يجود بمخزون أعواده على مراجع إلا بعد استجماع شرائط اربع:

الشريطة الأولى: كمال آلة الدّرك: من وفور العقل، وصفاء الذهن، وصحّة الغريزة، واتقاد القريحة، وحدة الخاطر، وجودة الذكاء والفطنة. فامّا الجاهل البليد، فهو عن مقاصد هذا الكتاب بعيد. وهذه شريطة غريزية، وقضية جبليّة، وهي من الله تعالى تحفة وهدية، ونعمة وعطية، لا تنال ببذل الجهد والاكتساب، وتنبتر دون دركها وسائل الاسبب.

ابو حامد محمد بن محمد الغزالي (٤٥٠–٥٠٥)

PREFACE

بسم الله الرّحمن الرّحيم

In the Name of Allah, Most Merciful and Compassionate

The texts of the Qur'ān and the *Sunnah* that prohibit *ribā* are not easy to understand. An earlier book written by this author, called *The Concept of Ribā and Islamic Banking*, appeared to be difficult for some readers. In fact, a few eager students stated that they were able to understand the text only after they had read it two or three times. This book tries to simplify some of the difficult areas of juristic interpretation. Some additional explanations have been added as compared to our last attempt in 1995, in the book mentioned.

A major problem has been the recognition, by modern ulama and scholars, of some basic truths about the prohibition of *ribā*. This non-recognition sometimes appears to be a reluctance to face a few harsh realities and a tendency to evade thorny issues. One such issue is the prohibition of all loans, other than what we have come to call a charitable loan or *qard ḥasan*. The issue lies at the heart of all Islamic banking. Instead of giving arguments on this issue and responding to the arguments made in favour of such prohibition, our modern scholars and leading muftis maintain total silence. The present book includes at least one instance of such evasion. It is only when a response on this issue is available from modern schoars that knowledge in this area will advance further. Without such a discussion, Islamic banking has very little chance of success.

Imran A. Nyazee
Islamabad
May, 2016

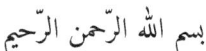

TABLE OF CONTENTS

Ch. 6 *Ṣarf, Qarḍ Ḥasan* and Contradictions in Modern Rulings

Ch. 8   Counting the *Fulūs* (Copper Coins) and Fiat Currency

Ch. 9   Conclusion About Islamic Banking

CHAPTER 1

INTRODUCTION: BACKGROUND TO THE CONFUSION ABOUT *RIBĀ*

من يرد الله به خيرا يفقّهه في الدين

He for whom God wills His blessings is granted the *fiqh* of *Dīn*

حديث شريف

1.1 The prohibtion of *ribā* (all imaginable forms of interest) is very clear in the Qur'ān and the *Sunnah*, yet a confusion exists in many minds about the true meaning of *ribā*. What are the causes of such confusion?

Ribā is prohibited by the texts of the Qur'ān and the *Sunnah*. This was the conclusion drawn unanimously by the Muslim jurists (*fuqahā'*); and it is also the decisive view of the vast majority of modern Muslim scholars. Despite this general agreement, a confusion persists in the minds of many, jurists and laymen alike, that even though some forms of interest are prohibited, the simple interest charged by banks may not be prohibited by Islamic law. Some find the concept of *ribā* very confusing when they cannot relate to the texts what the scholars say about the prohibition, and in the definitions they formulate for *ribā*. Further, when the scholars cannot convincingly answer questions about the "time-value of money in Islam," or when they cannot identify *ribā*-bearing modern transactions with ease, the confusion is aggravated. Consequently, Islamic banking appears to such persons to be based upon vague and slippery concepts. What is the reason for such doubts? Why do some uphold prohibition with conviction, while others do not?

The primary reason for the confusion, in our view, is that the method adopted by modern scholars in presenting the reasoning behind this issue is not very sound. They conclude rightly that *ribā*, and consequently bank-interest, is prohibited, but when they attempt to reason why it is prohibited, their views do not sound very convincing. The cause of this vagueness is that these scholars have neither presented their arguments for the prohibition of *ribā* in accordance with the methods of interpretation prescribed by the discipline of *uṣūl al-fiqh* nor have they tried to elaborate the work of the *fuqahā'* on the issue. Some have charted their own course in the area of interpretation, while others have assumed that the earlier jurists totally ignored those forms of transactions that we find identical to the transactions undertaken by banks today, especially the ordinary loan with interest transaction. Surprisingly, such assumptions about the work of the *fuqahā'* have been made by those who consider bank-interest to be legal and also by some of those who consider it prohibited.

The response to such an approach or assertion is that the *fuqahā'* were the lawyers and jurists of the dominant culture of their times, and they could not possibly ignore the most obvious cases of interest that were prevalent in commerce in those days; cases that are prevalent in commercial life to this day. They were, and still are, the leading authorities for the interpretation of the legal texts of the Qur'ān and the *Sunnah*. The views of the *fuqahā'* can only be understood if we attempt to understand the methods of interpretation employed by them for the resolution of this issue. Unfortunately, the methods of the *fuqahā'*, especially the earlier jurists, have been ignored in the discussions about *ribā* in the modern times.

1.2 Those who are responsible for creating this confusion may be classified into three categories.

1. **The first category includes those who reason on the basis of economics and the economic necessity of *ribā*.** They

argue on various grounds that modern economies cannot function without the economic tool of interest. They also assert that without interest modern banking is not possible. The task of the jurist is not to provide justifications or furnish rational foundations for the prohibition of interest. We, therefore, leave Muslim economists to engage in endless arguments with these people. These arguments can come to an end only when the *ribā*-free system is implemented and delivers the benefits that are associated with the Islamic system of distributive justice. Our task is to identify the law and make a programme for following it for Almighty Allah has said: "O ye who believe! Fear Allah, and give up what remains of your demand for usury, if ye are indeed believers. If ye do it not, take notice of war from Allah and His Messenger." [Qur'ān 2: 278, 279]

As for the argument of these people that interest is merely "rent on money" just like rent on other forms of capital so why should interest be singled out and prohibited, our response is as follows: **Rent on money is exactly what is prohibited by the Qur'ān and the *Sunnah*.** We will have occasion to show this in the following pages.

2. **The second category includes the well known Egyptian scholar Rashīd Riḍā and those who followed him.** Rashīd Riḍā maintained that simple interest is not prohibited, therefore, the Egyptian Post Office savings accounts, proposed in those days, were lawful. What is prohibited by the Qur'ān, he maintained, is just compound interest or interest "doubled and multiplied."[1] Rashīd Riḍā did not take into account the evidences as required by the discipline of *uṣūl al-fiqh*, and assumed that the texts and even the *fuqahā'* did not explicitly metnion loan with interest. We will describe his method briefly in what follows.

3. **The third category includes all modern scholars.** They

1. "O ye who believe! Devour not usury, doubled and multiplied; but fear Allah. that ye may (really) prosper." [Qur'ān 2 : 130]

rightly concluded that all forms of interest are prohibited. In their method of interpretation, however, they were under great pressure from the arguments given by Rashīd Riḍā. Rashīd Riḍā's writings led them to assume that the earlier jurists had not dealt clearly with the most common forms of interest known today; namely, interest on loans or bank interest.

The jurists, they concluded, were occupied more with a form of interest that they called "*ribā* of sales." This led them either to ignore the writings of the earlier jurists or not to give them due attention. The result is that when they explain the meaning of *ribā* on the basis of their reasoning, it does not sound very convincing. Further, when they frame definitions of *ribā,* these definitions cannot be directly related to the texts, and appear to be the work of their own minds. Consequently, this has given rise to some confusion about the issue of *ribā* and contradictions and problems in the implementation of the prohibition through Islamic banking.

With full respect for the sincerity of these scholars and their erudition, our request to them is not to "reinvent the wheel," but to go back to the writings of the earlier jurists, the *fuqahā'*, who are the leading legal minds of the Muslim world not only for their own times, but right up to this day. There is still time for doing so. It is only the adoption of the views of the *fuqahā'* that can lend authenticity to to the efforts being made to promote Islamic banking, and more importantly to make Islamic commerce a success. These few pages about the prohibition of *ribā* are, therefore, addressed to these scholars.

As this last category of scholars are also responsible for the decisions taken by the Islamic Fiqh Academy of the OIC, the decisions taken by the AOIFI, the *sharī'ah* boards, and their decisions have influenced the decisions of the Courts in Pakistan, our request applies to all these institutions as well: follow the method of the *fuqahā'* or, at least, respond to their reasoning with valid arguments.

1.3 Confusion about the prohibition of *ribā* will persist if the method of the *fuqahā'* is not followed, and it will prove to be a setback for Islamic banking.

The method of interpretation chosen by modern scholars has not only given rise to confusion about the issue, but has also led to some erroneous conclusions as well. These conclusions are creating contradictions during implementation. Accordingly:

1. The present form of Islamic banking will have no impact on the economy or the lives of the people, especially with respect to distributive justice.

2. The products designed and used for Islamic banking will continue to be based upon *rukhaṣ* (exemptions), or on a distorted form of *talfīq* (patchwork based upon two or more contracts) and this will give rise to a narrow and distorted form of conventional banking under the garb of Islamic banking.

3. The current form of Islamic banking will soon face a "famine" of new Islamic products and will be forced to declare conventional products as Islamic.

4. Consequently, the role of Islamic banking will continue to shrink and it will not even remain "parallel" banking as it is being termed today.

5. Ultimately, the present superficial differences between Islamic banking and conventional banking will disappear and what will remain will be conventional banking under a pseudonym.

1.4 The earlier jurists, the *fuqahā'*, are the leading authorities on the legal meanings in the Qur'ān and the *Sunnah*, and their works must be accorded the highest priority for all issues.

All *ijtihād* takes place within the texts of the Qur'ān and the *Sunnah*. Accordingly, the *fuqahā'* never move outside the texts, while undertaking *ijtihād*. Their minds and their legal reasoning are always governed by the texts of the Qur'ān and the *Sunnah*. Even when nothing is found in the texts, they rely upon principles derived from the Qur'ān and the *Sunnah* for new rulings. This way they ensure that the norms of the *sharī'ah* are observed and the intention of the Lawgiver followed. For any issue facing Muslims, the manuals of the *fuqahā'* must first be consulted for determining the legal meaning in the Qur'ān and the *Sunnah*. If the manuals of the *fuqahā'* do not provide an answer, the books called *Aḥkām al-Qur'ān* are to be followed. General *tafsīrs* may be approached only when the legal meaning cannot be determined from the first two sources. This order is recommended particularly for the courts in Pakistan.

1.5 The integral bond between the the Qur'ān and the *Sunnah* can never be severed during interpretation.

A permanent bond exists between the Qur'ān and the *Sunnah*, and this bond must be maintained during interpretation at all costs. To elaborate this point, we reproduce here some text from our book called *Islamic jurisprudence*.

The jurists maintain that the *Sunnah* is the second source among the sources of Islamic law. If the *mujtahid* does not find a text in the Qur'ān for a case he has to settle, he has recourse to the *Sunnah* for the derivation of the *ḥukm*. The evidence for this is the well known tradition of Mu'ādh ibn Jabal who was sent to

Yemen by the Prophet (pbuh). In addition to this there is the letter of 'Umar ibn al-Khaṭṭāb to Qāḍī Shurayḥ in which he instructs him to follow the Qur'ān first and then the *Sunnah*.

As regards the status of the *Sunnah* being secondary to the Qur'ān for proof of the *aḥkām*, the jurists maintain that the Qur'ān is definitive (*qaṭ'ī*) with respect to its narration in its details and as a whole, while the *Sunnah* is definitive as a whole, but not in all its details, because many of the reports are of the status of *khabar wāḥid*.

The *Sunnah* being an elaboration and commentary on the Qur'ān, it is not required to have recourse to it unless a text requires elaboration and commentary. If the text of the Qur'ān is explicit (*naṣṣ*) in its meaning it is to be acted upon, but if it is apparent (*ẓāhir*) having more than one meaning it is necessary to have recourse to its commentary, which is the *Sunnah*.

As the *Sunnah* is a primary source of law, the jurist has recourse to it for the derivation of the *aḥkām*; it is secondary and complementary to the Qur'ān. The authority of the *Sunnah* as a source of law is derived from the Qur'ān. The *aḥkām* derived from the *Sunnah* are, therefore, considered an explanation of the meanings in the Qur'ān. Even when the *Sunnah* appears exclusively to be dealing with a *ḥukm*, a close examination reveals that the *aḥkām* so revealed are based upon principles found in the Qur'ān and the *Sunnah* is merely extending the meaning of these principles or is linking up the rule with the principle. This may be elaborated in the following points:[2]

1. **The *Sunnah* is a commentary of the Qur'ān.** The *aḥkām* are often found in the Qur'ān in general, undetermined, or unelaborated form. The *Sunnah* restricts, qualifies, or elaborates these *aḥkām*.

   Examples of the *Sunnah* elaborating the unelaborated are like (1) the timings of prayer and their number as well as their *rak'as*; (2) elaboration of the kinds of wealth in which

2. The details of this discussion can be gleaned from an excellent discussion by al-Shāṭibī, *al-Muwāfaqāt*, vol. 4, 32 passim.

zakāt is to be paid and the amount to be paid in each as well as the time of obligation; (3) the case of *ribā*.

An example of the restriction of a general meaning is to be found in inheritance: "For the male two shares of the female." The *Sunnah* explains that the murderer will not inherit.

The example of elaboration is in the case of theft where the *Sunnah* elaborates the meaning saying that the property must be removed from the *ḥirz* and that it is the right hand that is to be cut.

2. **The *Sunnah* links a vacillating case with a known principle.** The *Sunnah* sometimes lays down rules that are not mentioned in the Qur'ān. These rules appear to be additions over the meanings in the Qur'ān and cannot be considered as elaborations or qualifications within the categories explained in the previous section. Some jurists, however, are of the opinion that a closer examination reveals that these rules are an elaboration in the sense of classifying a rule under a principle. Often a case vacillates between two principles and the *Sunnah* links up the case with one of these principles.

   For example, the Qur'ān has in a general way permitted all good things and has commanded the avoidance of *khabā'ith*. The *Sunnah* has linked with the *khabā'ith* the consumption of animals with molars and birds with claws, just as it has prohibited the consumption of domesticated donkeys.

   The Qur'ān has permitted the consumption of seafood and prohibited carrion. The dead fish in the sea vacillated between these two principles. The *Sunnah* linked it with permitted food: "Its water is pure and its *maytah* (carrion) is permissible."

   The Qur'ān permitted a slaughtered animal and prohibited carrion. The separated foetus of an animal after slaughter vacillated between the two principles. The *Sunnah* linked it with the slaughtered animal: "The slaughter of the mother amounts to the the slaughter of the foetus."

In these examples, we find that Qur'ān laid down two general principles, but there were certain cases that vacillated between them with the possibility of falling under either principle. The *Sunnah* attached the case to one of the general principles. Thus, the principle is mentioned in the Qur'ān and what appears to us as an additional rule laid down by the *Sunnah* is actually an instance of the principle. The function of the *Sunnah* here is the analytical development of the law.

3. **The *Sunnah* performs analogy on the basis of a rule in the Qur'ān.** The Qur'ān sometimes lays down a principle or a rule without elaborating all the categories falling under that principle or covered by the rule. The *Sunnah* links a resembling case with this rule, and this function appears to be similar to analogy.

   The Qur'ān prohibits marriage of two sisters to one man and then says that what is besides this is permitted. The cases of a woman along with her maternal or paternal aunt are also similar because of a common underlying cause. The *Sunnah*, therefore, prohibits such marriages too.

   The Qur'ān mentions that pure water descends from the sky and is preserved in the earth. The case of sea-water was not settled. The *Sunnah* declared that it is pure and even its carrion is lawful.

4. **The *Sunnah* lays down general principles.** The *Sunnah* sometimes lays down a general principle the individual categories of which have been mentioned by the Qur'ān. For example, the *Sunnah* lays down the principle: "No injury is to be caused or borne." The Qur'ān mentions a number of cases in which injury to others has been prohibited, like injury to a parents because of their child or injury to wives and so on. The prohibition of injury or harm is a general principle that is formulated by the *Sunnah*.

5. **The *Sunnah* elaborates the meaning of words in the Qur'ān.** An example of this the distinction of the white thread from the black thread during the month of Ramaḍān. The *Sunnah* explains that this is the light of day and the darkness of the night. The word *ribā*, as we will show, falls under this category.

In case the *Sunnah* does not provide the answer, the meaning has to be found in the practice of the Companions (God be pleased with them) and their opinions, which the Ḥanafī jurists consider a binding source of law. If there is a need after all this, references may be provided from other religions, history and so on, but these are not binding.

1.6 The methodology indicated has a definite impact on legal meanings, and this is especially true for the meaning of *ribā*.

The methodology described above is always followed by the jurists. For example, the literal meanings of the terms *ṣalāt* (prayer), *zakāt* (poor-due) and *sariqah* (theft) are known. So is the literal meaning of the term *ribā* (excess). All the details of *ṣalāt, zakāt* and *sariqah* have, however, come from the *Sunnah,* as indicated above. There has never been a need to say that: this is the *ṣalāt* of the Qur'ān and this the *ṣalāt* of the *Sunnah*; this is the *zakāt* of the Qur'ān and this the *zakāt* of the *Sunnah*; this is the form of *sariqah* stated in the Qur'ān and this form in the *Sunnah*. ***In the same way, there is no need to say that this is the ribā of the Qur'ān and this is the ribā of the Sunnah. Both the Qur'ān and the Sunnah deal with all forms of ribā. Separation is not possible and the earlier fuqahā' did not separate them as that would amount to cutting the bond between the Qur'ān and the Sunnah, thus, arriving at doubtful conclusions.*** Modern scholars separated *ribā* of the Qur'ān from *ribā* of the *Sunnah*. There was no need to do so, as we will show. ***This is the heart of the problem, the source of all confusion, the biggest hurdle standing in the way of true Islamic commerce.***

We may now move to the gradual resolution of this problem and try to remove the confusion through measured steps.

CHAPTER 2

THE SOURCE OF CONFUSION

We may state at the outset that a major part of this chapter has been borrowed from our earlier book on *ribā* called *The Concept of Ribā and Islamic Banking*.

2.1 Most modern interpretations are based upon a selective reading of the views of the famous jurist Abū Bakr al-Jaṣṣāṣ, and thereafter the views of Fakhr al-Dīn al-Rāzī.

In all fairness to modern scholars, their views are not totally unfounded. They based their opinions on the writings of some earlier scholars, but these were works on *aḥkām al-Qur'ān* or general *tafsīrs*. **The views were not based upon the authentic manuals of *fiqh*, which is the proper thing to do as indicated above. Further, in some cases, a few statements were picked out of context and the whole text was not quoted.**

Abū Bakr al-Jaṣṣāṣ, one of the earliest and very famous Ḥanafī jurist said:

> The *ribā* that was known to the Arabs and was practiced by them was the lending (*qarḍ*) of *dirhams* and *dīnārs* for a period with an excess in proportion to what was lent and on which they had agreed. They were not acquainted with the spot sale when it contained an excess of the same genus.[3]

3. Al-Jaṣṣās, *Aḥkām al-Qur'ān*, vol. 1, 465. Here "spot sale" refers to the tradition of the six commodities that will be coming up later.

This statement by al-Jaṣṣāṣ was then picked up by Fakhr al-Dīn al-Rāzī, the author of *Tafsīr Kabīr*. He said:

> Know that *ribā* is of two kinds: *ribā al-nasī'ah* and *ribā al-faḍl*. *Ribā al-nasī'ah* was well known and familiar during the *jāhilīyah*. This was so because they used to give wealth on the condition that they would take a fixed amount each month, while the principal amount still remained. Thereafter, when it was time for the repayment of the debt, they demanded the principal from the debtor. If he was unable to pay, they increased the claim and the period. This is the *ribā* that they used to practice. ...As for *ribā* through the spot transaction (*ribā al-naqd*), it is the sale of wheat for flour made from it, or what is similar.[4]

This statement became the inspiration for Rashīd Riḍā's views outlined in the next section. Al-Rāzī, however, went further and also said the following:

> On the other hand, His words, "prohibited *ribā*," include a specific type of contract that they used to conclude as *ribā*. This was *ribā al-nasī'ah*. Thus, His words, "prohibited *ribā*," apply exclusively to *nasī'ah* and it is, therefore, established that His words "Allāh has permitted sale," include the spot sale and His words, "prohibited *ribā*," do not include it, which necessarily implies that it is permitted.... As for the majority of the *mujtahids*, they agreed about the prohibition of *ribā* in both kinds: the first kind by the Qur'ān, and the second by the *Sunnah*."[5]

This view was repeated by Shāh Walī Allāh. It is in the light of these statements that Abū Zahrah and Mawlāna abul 'Alā'

4. Fakhr al-Dīn al-Rāzī, *al-Tafsīr al-Kabīr*, vol. 7, 91.
5. Ibid. 92. As we will show later, even this view of al-Rāzī does not mean that the *ribā* of the Qur'ān is the loan transaction and the *ribā* of the *Sunnah* is merely *faḍl*.

Mawdūdī made the statements that we have quoted two sections after this.

These quotations set the stage for the views, first, of Rashīd al-Riḍā and then those of modern scholars.

2.2 Rashīd Riḍā declared simple interest to be legal; only compound interest "doubled and multiplied" was prohibited in his view.

The first approach was that of Rashīd Riḍā of Egypt, the student of Imām 'Abduh, the Mufti of Egypt. Rashīd Riḍā, it must be acknowledged, was a great scholar. He had a great command over the methods used by the earlier authors of *tafsīrs*. He came up, however, with an interpretation of the problem of *ribā* that was different from the one adopted by the *fuqahā'*.[6] In expressing his views on the issue of *ribā*, he not only put forward a new opinion, but also influenced the methods of interpretation used by those who upheld his view later as well as of those who opposed him. For building his opinion, he took the cue mostly from the words of al-Rāzī quoted in the previous section giving them a meaning that was most probably not intended by al-Rāzī.

6. Most of what we have stated in this book about the views of Rashīd Riḍā is borrowed from the book of Zakī al-Dīn Badawī, *Naẓarīyat al-Ribā al-Muḥarram*. Badawī was working on a project for the Islamization of laws alongwith Dr. al-Sanhūrī. At that time his opinion was similar to Dr. Sanhūri's opinion or that of Rashīd Riḍā. Thus, he had maintained that simple interest charged at the banks is not prohibited. He later changed his opinion and held that interest of all kinds is *ribā* and is prohibited. Expressing his opinion in his book on the prohibition of *ribā*, he fully discussed and documented the views of Rashīd Riḍā including opinions attributed to Muḥammad 'Abduh. I would like to acknowledge that his book helped me understand the views and reasoning of Rashīd Riḍā through a systematic and well presented account. Those who are interested in this controversy should have recourse to Zakī al-Dīn Badawī's book now available in translation.

1. ***Ribā* in the Qur'ān and *ribā* in the *Sunnah*—distinguished.** Rashīd Riḍā made a distinction between the rules of *ribā* laid down in the texts of the Qur'ān and those laid down in the *Sunnah*. He maintained that the primary form of *ribā* is prohibited by the Qur'ān, and this prohibition is to be maintained at all times. He insisted, on the other hand, that the texts of the *Sunnah* prohibit a lighter or secondary type of *ribā*, which is generally prohibited, but may be permitted in case of necessity (*ḍarūrah*).[7]

2. ***Ribā al-jāhilīyah* as *ribā* of the Qur'ān**. To discover the meaning of the primary form of *ribā*, which in his view was prohibited by the Qur'ān alone, he first examined the literal meaning of the term *ribā* for which he relied mostly upon the writings of the commentators of the Qur'ān rather than on the works of the jurists.[8] He said that this form of *ribā* was called *ribā al-jāhilīyah*, which was prohibited not only by the Qur'ān, but expressly by the Prophet (God's peace and blessings be upon him) during the Farewell Pilgrimage.[9] The primary form of *ribā*, therefore, was the *ribā* that the Qur'ān describes as one charged "doubled and multiplied," in proportion to the principal amount of the debt or loan.

3. ***Ribā al-nasī'ah* and *bay' al-nasī'ah*.** For describing the details of this form of *ribā*—that is, the type prohibited by the Qur'ān—he again relied upon the commentators. Referring to the writings of these commentators, he tried to show that in the initial stage of the contemplated usurious transaction (or contract) no *ribā* was stipulated, because the transaction

7. Apparently, he relied upon the views of Ibn al-Qayyim for this opinion.
8. It is true that some of these commentators, like Fakhr al-Dīn Rāzī, were also well known jurists, but it is to be kept in mind that when such writers deal with *fiqh* their style and method of presentation is different, because they are addressing jurists, while in their commentaries they are addressing the generalist.
9. In this he may be said to have followed the opinion of Ibn Rushd, who we may add is to be considered a later jurist.

was a credit sale (usually referred to as *bay' al-nasī'ah*, that is, sale with a period of delay),[10] and any excess that there may have been was included in the enhanced price of the product itself. A credit sale is one where the buyer acquires the goods sold and promises to pay later after a determined period. It is to be expected that the seller in such a case will charge a slightly higher price than he would if the payment was made in cash. Thus, the seller and the buyer used to agree upon a period within which the payment would be made and the excess in price was not stipulated separately.

Increase at the end of the period of payment. When this period was over the seller demanded his money from the buyer saying: "Will you pay or increase the amount due in lieu of further delay." In case they agreed upon a further delay, the buyer not being in a position to pay or not wanting to pay for some other reason, the amount due would be increased or even doubled. When this process went on for a few more periods of delay, the original sum stood "doubled and multiplied." The Arabic word for delay in transactions is *nasī'ah*, and this form of *ribā* was designated as *ribā al-nasī'ah* prohibited by the Qur'ān,[11] according to Rashīd Riḍā

10. Also referred to as *bay' mu'ajjal*.
11. I will show later that it may not be proper to designate the entire transaction of *ribā* with the title *ribā al-nasī'ah*.

relying on al-Rāzī and others.

Rashīd Riḍā's Conclusion

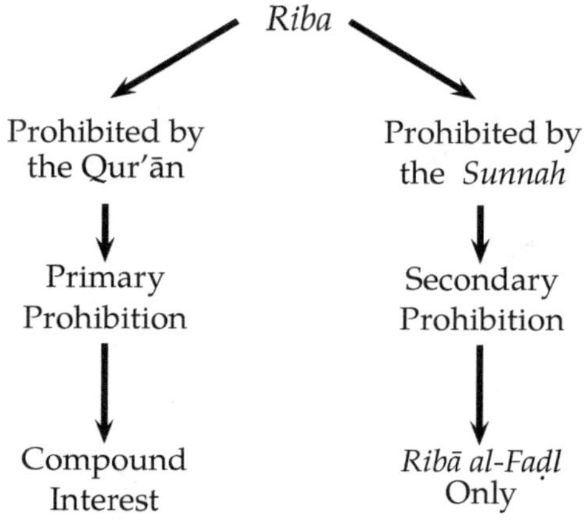

***Ribā* doubled and multiplied is not the same as interest on savings accounts.** This transaction, that is, doubling and redoubling of the amount, Rashīd Riḍā maintained, may be described as compound interest, but it does not cover the simple interest charged on loans by banks or paid by banks to their depositors. Further, in this transaction the excess was not stipulated in the first period of delay when the commodity was bought, but in the second and subsequent extensions of the period. Since the excess was not stipulated in the initial transaction, the transaction could not be termed usurious for the initial period; that is, it became usurious through the extension of the periods in lieu of doubling or redoubling.

4. ***Ribā al-nasā'*.** The *Sunnah,* he maintained, prohibited other forms of transactions and along with these it prohibited the same kind of *nasī'ah* prohibited by the Qur'ān. To identify *ribā* in delayed transactions contemplated by the *Sunnah* the word used was *nasā'*, which also means delay. This was held to be specific to sales and did not apply to

loans, which were covered by *ribā al-nasī'ah* prohibited by the Qur'ān.

Ribā al-faḍl. The remaining proscriptions in the *Sunnah* were directed at a peculiar kind of transaction, unknown to the Arabs before this. This pertained to sales. It was the excess (*faḍl*) found in one of the counter-values through weight, measure, or count, when the two counter-values belonged to the same species and were being exchanged on the spot, at once. Thus, for example, if two persons were exchanging gold with each other, the amount of gold must be equal in weight on both sides and the two quantities must change hands on the spot, at once. The reason why it was said that this transaction was unknown to the Arabs is that it is difficult to conceive why two persons would exchange equal quantities of the same commodity at once. This type of *ribā* he, along with everyone else, called *ribā al-faḍl*. Relying upon the writings of some of the later jurists he maintained that this type of *ribā* is lighter or secondary and may be permitted in cases of necessity (*ḍarūrah*).[12] For example, Imām Mālik permitted a battalion of soldiers leaving on a mission in a hurry to pay gold at the mint and take *dīnārs* in return even if the weight of the *dīnārs* was less than the gold paid.

5. **Primary form of prohibition.** To further strengthen his view that *ribā al-nasī'ah* prohibited by the Qur'ān is the only form that is primarily prohibited, having shown earlier that it means compound interest alone, he relied upon the tradition and views reported from Ibn 'Abbās (God be pleased with them both). The words of one version of the tradition are: "Verily, *ribā* is in *nasī'ah*." This could mean that the other form, that is *faḍl*, is not the primary form of *ribā*. It is reported that relying upon this Ibn 'Abbās permitted, for example, the sale of three standardized *dirhams* for two standardized *dirhams* when these were exchanged immediately,

12. 'Abd al-Razzāq al-Sanhūrī also maintains the same view. He reasons on the basis of the views of Ibn al-Qayyim. See *Maṣādir al-Ḥaqq*, vol. 3, 237, 241.

that is, not with a delay from either side showing that it was only delay that was prohibited and not simple excess.

6. **Only compound interest prohibited.** The conclusion to be drawn from all this was that the only form of *ribā* that is strictly prohibited, and prohibited by the Qur'ān, is one that leads to the doubling and multiplying of the principal amount. This was held to be equivalent to compound interest. The other forms of *ribā*, he held, are not primarily prohibited and an exemption may be provided from them if required by the principle of necessity. **Simple interest charged or paid by the banks, he maintained, was not prohibited by the provisions of the Qur'ān at all nor by those of the *Sunnah*.**

7. **Muḥammad 'Abduh.** Some of these views were attributed to his teacher, Imām 'Abduh, by Rashīd Riḍā, but there are scholars who maintain that these were his own opinions mixed up with the views of 'Abduh. The point is not important as far as the argument is concerned.

8. **Rashīd Riḍā's following.** The views expressed by Rashīd Riḍā led to other opinions of a similar nature. The result was that the Egyptian law, taking into account the sentiments of the people, focused on the eradication of compound interest in certain cases, but it did not prohibit simple interest. Details of this are to be found in the writings of 'Abd al-Razzāq al-Sanhūrī, the well known Egyptian scholar.[13]

9. **Rashīd Riḍā's method.** Later writers, who maintain that bank interest is not prohibited, not being covered by the Qur'ānic provisions about *ribā*, generally follow the line of reasoning adopted by Rashīd Riḍā.

13. Ibid. vol. 3, 176–249

2.3 The main points emerging from Rashīd Riḍā's analysis are five.

The following are the main points emerging from the writings of Rashīd Riḍā insofar as they are relevant to our discussion:

1. *Ribā* is of two types: *ribā* of the Qur'ān and *ribā* of the *Sunnah.*

2. *Ribā* of the Qur'ān is the *ribā* of the Jahiliyyah, that is, *ribā* that was charged "doubled and multiplied," by stipulation not at the beginning of the contract, but at the end of the first period for the second period of further delay agreed upon. It may arise from the credit sale as well, that is, it is stipulated for seeking further delay, if payment cannot be made when it is due. This is prohibited in his view by the Qur'ān.

3. Simple interest charged or paid by the banks is not included in the meaning of *ribā* of the Qur'ān, and is lawful. It is not prohibited.

4. *Ribā* of the Qur'ān, "doubled and multiplied" may also be called *ribā al-nasī'ah,* as it involves delay; the word *nasī'ah* means delay.

5. *Ribā* of the *Sunnah* applies to sales, and when it deals with delay such delay is called *nasā'*. When it deals with excess that can be weighed or measured such *ribā* is called *ribā al-faḍl* or *ribā* of excess in a spot transaction.

2.4 A very important link between modern scholars and Rashīd Riḍā is 'Abd al-Razzāq al-Sanhūri.

'Abd al-Razzāq al-Sanhūri, the well know Egyptian lawyer, who undertook a detailed study of Islamic law, especially on *ribā*. Dr. al-Sanhūrī classified the types of *ribā* in a slightly different manner. He is conscious of the discrepancy between the views of the earlier jurists and those of Rashīd Riḍā. Finding it difficult to classify *ribā al-nasī'ah*, he says:

> If the manifest (*jalī*) form of *ribā* according to Ibn al-Qayyim is *ribā al-jāhilī*, which is the first type, and the lighter (concealed) form of *ribā* is *ribā al-faḍl*, which is the third type, then, where do we place *ribā al-nasī'ah*, which occurs in the noble *ḥadīth*? Is it the manifest (*jalī*) form of *ribā* that is to be linked with *ribā al-jāhilīyah*? Or is it the concealed (lighter) form of *ribā* that is to be linked with *ribā al-faḍl*? It is obvious that Ibn al-Qayyim links it—without expressly saying so—with *ribā al-jāhilīyah* and considers it a manifest form of *ribā* like it. Thus, when he speaks of *ribā al-nasī'ah*, considering it the manifest form of *ribā*, he intends thereby both *ribā al-jāhilīyah* and *ribā al-nasī'ah* that is mentioned in the *ḥadīth*.[14]

It appears that this view of al-Sanhūrī led both Abū Zahrah and Mawlāna Mawdūdī to classify *ribā al-nasī'ah* as *ribā al-jāhilīyah*, that is, the *ribā* of the Qur'ān. Al-Sanhūrī himself did not do so. He considered *ribā al-nasī'ah* to be of the same lighter category as *ribā al-faḍl*. This he attributed to Rashīd Riḍā.[15] The *ribā* of the Qur'ān in his view was only *ribā al-jāhilī*. The *ribā* of traditions in his view was permitted in case of mere need, while the *ribā* of the Qur'ān was permitted in case of necessity. He made a distinction between need and necessity saying that necessity was similar to the consumption of carrion under duress (state of *iḍṭirār*).

Al-Sanhūrī's views add to the confusion surrounding the issue of *ribā* in the writings of modern scholars.

14. Al-Sanhūrī, *Maṣādir*, vol. 3, 218.
15. Ibid. 219

2.5 Modern scholars followed Rashīd Riḍā and al-Sanhūrī, but altered a few basic assumptions.

Modern scholars maintain that all forms of interest, including simple interest charged by the banks, are prohibited. This is the generally accepted view, and it conforms with the views of the jurists. The only problem is that these writers, like Rashīd Riḍā:

(a) Begin with the explanation of the literal meaning of the term trying to determine its various manifestations from the writings of the commentators of the Qur'ān.

(b) They, again like Rashīd Riḍā, make a distinction between *ribā* prohibited by the Qur'ān and *ribā* prohibited by the *Sunnah.*

(c) They designate the first form as *ribā al-nasī'ah,* the primary form of prohibition, and maintain that it is prohibited by the Qur'ān. They designate it with its other name too, that is, *ribā al-jāhilīyah.*

(d) They insist that *ribā al-jāhilīyah* includes interest on loans, whether it is simple or compound, and whether it is charged by banks or by someone else. This is what al-Jaṣṣāṣ maintained.

(e) They designate the form of *ribā* prohibited by the *Sunnah* as *ribā al-faḍl* and maintain that this is a secondary form of prohibition pertaining to the eradication of barter.[16]

(f) In short, they prohibit *ribā,* **in its various forms, without fully identifying the meaning of *ribā* or the transactions of *ribā* in the texts of the Qur'ān and the *Sunnah.***

16. This strange view is advocated by an economist.

Views of Modern Scholars

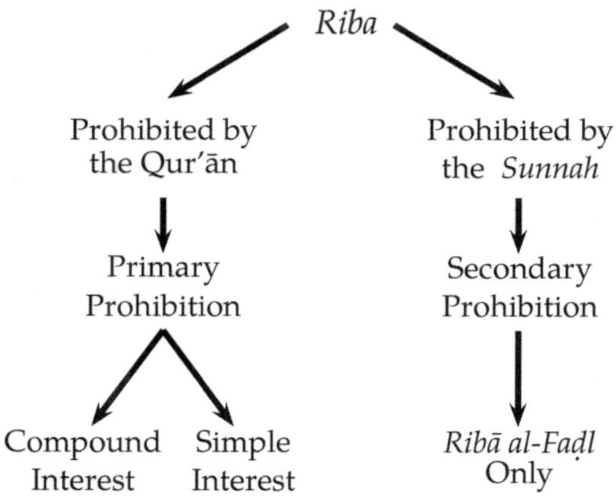

The conclusion drawn by modern scholars is almost the same as that drawn by the earlier jurists, but it is the method of interpretation followed by these scholars that causes confusion, for which reason the insistence of these scholars upon the prohibition of bank interest does not sound very convincing to some. That these scholars agree with the first approach with respect to the distinction between the forms of *ribā* prohibited by the Qur'ān and those prohibited by the *Sunnah* can be seen from the words of Abū Zahrah, who was a well known jurist in Egypt. He said:

> Before we put down the pen, we will discuss the legal issue related to *ribā,* which is that the excess in lieu of the period [of repayment] is the *ribā* of *jāhiliyah.* It is also called *ribā al-nasī'ah,* because the excess in it is in lieu of the period, that is, the duration of delay. The scholars are all in agreement about its prohibition, and it is the *ribā* of the Qur'ān.... There is a technical form of *ribā* or that of the Islamic usage. This is the *ribā* of sales (*ribā al-buyū'*).[17]

17. Foreword to Zakī al-Dīn Badawī, *Naẓarīyat al-Ribā al-Muḥarram* (Cairo: 1940).

He goes on to show that *ribā* of sales is prohibited by the *Sunnah*. His view on exemption due to necessity from the provision of *ribā* in the *Sunnah* appears to be no different from that of Rashīd Riḍā. He says:

> It is a settled matter in *fiqh* that a primary prohibition is not made permissible except under duress, and there can be no absolute duress that would permit the consumption of interest. A secondary (*li-ghayrihi*) prohibition, however, may be permitted in the case of need. Thus, if one is facing an acute need for borrowing on interest, because he cannot find anyone who would grant him a *qarḍ ḥasan*, then, Allāh would remove the sin from him, and associate two sins with one who does not grant a loan except on interest. If, therefore, a state is faced with an acute need for a loan with interest, because she cannot find another way to satisfy her needs, then, it is to be hoped that Allāh will forgive those who do so.[18]

A closer examination of this statement reveals that the secondary or *li-ghayrihi* prohibition is not confined to what he has referred to as the *ribā* of sales in the previous quotation, which was declared permissible in case of necessity by Rashīd Riḍā. He goes further and permits Muslim states to indulge in the primary form of *ribā*, if interest-free loans are not available. In this he appears to be following Dr. al-Sanhūrī.

In cases other than necessity, the only difference between the conclusions drawn by Rashīd Riḍā and Abū Zahrah, then, turns on the legality or illegality of simple interest charged at the banks.

The distinction between the forms of *ribā* prohibited by the Qur'ān and those prohibited by the *Sunnah*, is also made by the learned Sayyid Abul 'Alā Mawdūdī. He describes *ribā al-nasī'ah* as follows:

---

18. Ibid. Al-Sarakhsī maintains that need does not permit *ribā*, because a need can be met without the commission of *ḥarām*. *Al-Mabsūṭ*, vol. 14, 7.

> We have stated earlier that *ribā*, in fact, is that excess or *fā'idah* which a creditor receives from the debtor as a stipulated excess over and above the principal amount. In the terminology of the law, this is called *ribā al-nasī'ah*. Thus, it is *ribā* that is paid and received in a loan transaction. It is this *ribā* that has been prohibited by the Qur'ān. The whole *Ummah* agrees about its prohibition.[19]

As distinguished from this form of *ribā*, which is prohibited by the Qurān, he describes *ribā al-faḍl* as a form of *ribā* prohibited by the *Sunnah*:

> *Ribā al-faḍl* is the excess that is found in the spot exchange of two things of the same genus. The Messenger of Allāh (p.b.u.h.) has prohibited this form.[20]

This is the same view as that of Abū Zahrah. Thus, some of the leading scholars of this century make a distinction between the type of *ribā* prohibited by the Qur'ān, which they designate as *ribā al-nasī'ah*, and the type of *ribā* prohibited by the *Sunnah*, which they call *ribā al-faḍl*.

We have quoted just two of the leading scholars of the last century; namely, Abū Zahrah and Abū al-'Alā Mawdūdī. The fact, however, is that all modern scholars, without exception, uphold these views. These views are also held by all the Islamic institutions today. This is natural as the institutions rely on these scholars. The institutions include the Islamic Fiqh Academy of the OIC, the Accounting and Auditing Organisation of Islamic Financial Institutions (AOIFI), all the *sharī'ah* boards of Islamic banks and central banks. In addition to this, the same view has been advanced in the two famous judgements of the Courts in Pakistan (FSC and SC).

19. Abul 'Alā Mawdūdī, *Sūd* (Lahore, 1989), 163.
20. Ibid. 65.

2.6 If all modern scholars unanimously uphold a view, why should we try to question or alter such a view?

The response to this important question is that such a view does not deal comprehensively with the issue of *riba*. This leads to two problems:

(a) The main problem is that by focusing on the text of the Qur'ān alone and not linking it to the texts of the *Sunnah* or not seeking elaboration from the *Sunnah*, the two categories of scholars have arrived at two different conclusions. Rashīd Riḍā relying more on Fakhr al-Dīn Rāzī's statement comes to the conclusion that **bank interest is not prohibited.** Modern scholars, using the same methodology, and relying more on Abū Bakr al-Jaṣṣāṣ's statement come to the conclusion that **bank interest is prohibited.** The disagreement itself gives rise to some kind of confusion (*shubhah*) in the understanding of the concept of *ribā*. That also shows that these two types of opinions are based merely on the words of some of the earlier writers and are not really linked to the texts.

(b) The second problem concerns implementation of the opinions to carry out Islamic banking. Not seeking the elaboration of the texts of the Qur'ān from the *Sunnah* has led to incomplete implementation of the prohibition of *ribā*. Showing this is the burden of this book. ***We will show why the prohibition of ribā cannot be applied in its totality and with what consequences.***

Further, the methodology of modern scholars (if they have a methodology of interpretation) does not conform to the authentic and tested methodology of the earlier jurists. It ignores the concept of *bayān* and does not give due importance to the integral bond between the Qur'ān and the *Sunnah*, as discussed above. There is, therefore, a need to show what results are arrived at through the authentic methodology of the *fuqahā'*.

As the *fuqahā'* do not talk in terms of loans, and instead focus on the rules, it has been assumed that they ignored loans. Others like Rashīd Riḍā have assumed that Islamic law does not even talk about loans, because loans with interest are permitted. This is not a point that can be ignored. The reason is that it has been taken up as an argument in the review petition filed before the Supreme Court of Pakistan. Counsel advanced the argument that Islamic law is not concerned with loans and consequently with interest on such loans. The case has now been sent back to the Federal Shariat court and this issue is likely to come up whenever the case comes up for hearing.

More important than the above is the fact that the definitions framed by modern scholars and the conclusions drawn by them about *ribā* are not precise. As a result some contradictions have started appearing in their own *fatwas* and further contradictions are likely to arise if remedial action is not taken. This shows that as the basic rules have not been identified, it is becoming exceedingly difficult to identy modern *ribā*-bearing transactions. Other reasons that are likely to affect the programme of Islamic banking have been recorded earlier. The cumulative effect may be that the structure of Islamic banking erected so far can come crashing down or it may very soon turn into conventional banking and remain Islamic in name alone.

Finaly, the most important and crucial reason is that the method used by modern scholars cannot recognise all forms or *ribā* and hence all the transactions of *ribā*. It is only the method of the jurists that does so, and has a tremendous impact on the nature of the transactions prohibited.

The method adopted by modern scholars separates the evidences and sets aside some of them, just because they cannot explain them or absorb them within their method. Take the case of the tradition of 'Ubādah ibn al-Ṣāmit (R). They just push it away by saying that this applies to sales, and is a minor form of *ribā*; they have no basis for saying so. Further, they have never paused to reflect as to which evidence directly supports the claims they make and the definitions they attempt to give.

The purpose of this study is to present arguments to modern scholars from *fiqh* literature so that they may carefully consider them and adopt the position that is legally sound.

2.7 The assertion of modern scholars that *ribā al-nasī'ah* is prohibited by the Qur'ān, while *ribā al-faḍl* is prohibited by the *Sunnah*, is conceptually incorrect and based on flawed reasoning resulting from a lack of appreciation of the texts (even though they conclude that interest on loans is prohibited)—this reasoning has led to distortions as far as the concept of *ribā* and Islamic banking are concerned.

We would like to state the problem at the outset in precise terms (we have already stated the problem in § 6 in the previous chapter). Modern scholars, after having been confused by Rashīd Riḍā, came to the conclusion that interest in loan transactions is called *ribā al-nasī'ah,* and this form is prohibited by the Qur'ān. They made this assertion, because they did not find the loan transaction mentioned explicitly by the jurists (that is, as our economists understand it today). They did not appreciate the traditions and the rules of *ribā* in the *Sunnah* and said that *ribā* described by the *Sunnah* is *ribā al-faḍl*. To add to the confusion, some economists who pretended to have expertise in *fiqh* made preposterous statements. For example, one such economist said that the traditions are merely trying to "discourage barter." One can do nothing but feel frustrated by such expositions of an issue that has been clearly stated and elaborated by the jurists; and about which they have never disagreed throughout the history of *fiqh*.

It will be our task in this book to show that this assertion, as well as the reasoning, upon which the claim is based are both false. We will also show why it is damaging and distorting *fiqh*.

2.8 Some persons who are making attempts to add further to the confusion are claiming, naively, that there was no *ijmā'* (consensus) on the meaning of *ribā*.

The assertions stem from a the lack of a comprehensive understanding of the meaning of *ribā* and that of *ijmā*. *Ijmā* takes place on a point about which there is confusion or that has more than one meaning. The prohibition of *ribā* is definitive (*qaṭ'ī*) and does not need *ijmā'* for its support. If consensus here is supposed to mean disagreement by a few then we would say that there has never been any jurist in the history of Islamic law who has said that *ribā* is not prohibited. It is true that modern scholars may have disagreed, along with some economists, but that is a different matter.

Yes, there might be disagreement about minor individual transactions, like exchanging two animals for one, or whether *ribā* runs in the sale of bread and meat, but the general prohibition stands undisputed. Such a prohibition does not need *ijmā'* to strengthen it. There was a slight disagreement based on the statement of Ibn 'Abbās (God be pleased with him), "Verily, *ribā* runs in *nasī'ah* (delay)," whether *ribā* exists in a spot transaction of the same currency. This was confusion was removed and consensus was achieved right in the period of the Companions (God be pleased with them). We may quote al-Sarakhsī, who says, in the *Book of Ṣarf*, that there is complete consensus on this point as well:

> From this we come to know that there is total consensus on the prohibition of excess (*tafāḍul*) in the first period and the judgement of a *qāḍī* that goes against this is null and void.

This might raise the question whether the Federal Shariat Court or the Shariat Appellate Bench can reopen the issue of the prohibition of *ribā*? We may now turn to the meaning of *ribā* as it is found in the texts and has been elaborated by the jurists of Islam.

CHAPTER 3

THE MEANING OF *RIBĀ* ACCORDING TO THE JURISTS

To understand the concept of *ribā,* as elaborated by the *fuqahā',* a clear statement must first be made about the position taken by the *fuqahā'* and then a few basic ideas must be clarified. The statement may be compared with what we have stated in § 12 above. The statement will be followed by a detailed analysis.

THE POSITION TAKEN BY THE EARLIER JURISTS

1. **When delay (*nasī'ah* or *nasā'*) and excess (*faḍl*) exist in the same transaction (for example the loan transaction), with *faḍl* being in lieu of *nasī'ah,* the transaction is prohibited by both the Qur'ān and the Sunnah.**
2. **When delay (*nasī'ah*) exists alone in a transaction, it is prohibited by the *Sunnah.***
3. **When excess (*faḍl*) exists alone in a transaction, it is prohibited by the *Sunnah.***
4. **As the *Sunnah* is an elaboration of the Qur'ān, what is prohibited by the *Sunnah* is also prohibited by the Qur'ān, for the *Sunnah* is elaborating the meanings in the Qur'ān.**
5. **The crucial factor in all such transactions is delay (*nasī'ah* or *nasā'*), for it deals with the time-value of money, of which the jurists were well aware.**

It will be our endeavour to show that **not only are these statements in conformity with the texts, but they also explain all forms of transacions that bear *ribā* and are consequently prohibited.** This is not a mere rearrangement of words or stating the same thing again: the impact of these statements affects the heart of Islamic banking and is meant to bring out its true nature that has not been understood so far. We may now begin with basic ideas and build on them to elaborate the rules derived by the jurists.

3.1 Modern scholars have completely ignored significant statements from Abū Bakr al-Jaṣṣāṣ and relied only on a parital reading of his text. He never meant that *ribā* of the Qur'ān is different from *ribā* of the Sunnah. Further, there is no difference between the terms *nasī'ah* and *nasā'*; both mean delay and not *ribā* arising out of delay.

Jaṣṣāṣ never meant what has been attributed to him by modern scholars. We will quote the rest of the text from al-Jaṣṣāṣ to show that he was true to the method of the *fuqahā'*. He says:

The term ribā became a technical term of the law:

> In the law (*shar'*), it (*ribā*) is applied to meanings in which it was not used in the language. This is indicated by the fact that the Prophet (God's peace and blessings be upon him) termed *nasā'* as *ribā* in the tradition of Usāmah ibn Zayd. He said, "Verily, *ribā* is in *nasī'ah*" ....[21] It is established from this that *ribā* became a technical term, for had it been governed by its original meaning in the language, it would not have been obscure for 'Umar (R), who was fully aware of the names used in the language, being a native speaker.

The technical term includes transactions not known to the Arabs, therefore, the word ribā used in the Qur'ān needs further elaboration from the Sunnah:

21. Note that the terms *nasā'* and *nasī'ah* have been used as synonyms.

> This (the conversion of the word into a technical meaning) is also indicated by the fact that the Arabs were not aware of the sale of gold for gold and silver for silver with a delay (*nasā'*) as *ribā*, but this is *ribā* in the technical meaning. If this (meaning of *ribā*) is as we have explained it, then, it became like all the other unelaborated (*mujmal*) words that are in need of an elaboration (*bayān*). These are terms that have been transferred from the language to the law and assigned meanings to which the word was not originally applied in the language, like *ṣalāt*, *ṣawm*, and *zakāt*. Such words are in need of a *bayān* and it is not proper to employ them in legal reasoning for the prohibition of any of the contracts, unless an evidence has been adduced to show that such a meaning is employed by the law (*shar'*).

Here Jaṣṣāṣ makes three important statements:

1. First, he uses the terms *nasā'* and *nasī'ah* interchangeably. There is no difference between the two terms according to the *fuqahā*.

2. After the description in the Qur'ān and the *Sunnah*, both sources assign a technical meaning to *ribā*. It is this meaning that is now relevant for the law and not the literal meaning.

3. The word *ribā* as used in the Qur'ān is *mujmal* (unelaborated). It is in need of elaboration from the *Sunnah*. This view is also held by other jurists like Sarakhsī, Bazdawī and others. Only an ignoramus, who has superficial knowledge of Islamic law, will conclude that it is not *mujmal*. This means that it is the *Sunnah* and *Sunnah* alone that will determine the entire meaning of the the term *ribā*. Separating the meanings in the Qur'ān from those in the *Sunnah* is incorrect.

He says further that the entire and total meaing of the term *ribā* is determined by two evidences taken together. His statement is:

> All these were then accomodated under the prohition of the words, "And prohibited *ribā*," because of the term having included them all in its meaning assigned by the law (*shar'*). Their dealings in *ribā* were nothing more than the lending (*qarḍ*) of *dirhams* or *dīnārs* with a stipulated excess for a period.

And the tradition he mentions in his conclusive statement:

> Thus, **all that the term *ribā* in the law comprises is included in *nasā'* (delay) and *tafāḍul*** (excess through estimation) in accordance with conditions that are deemed established by the *fuqahā'*. The evidence for this is the saying of the Prophet (God's peace and blessings be upon him): "Wheat for wheat, like for like, from hand to hand, and the excess is *ribā*; barley for barley, like for like, from hand to hand, and the excess is *ribā*." He also mentioned dates, salt, gold, and silver, and termed *faḍl* in the same species of wheighed and measured things as *ribā*.

Thus, it is these two evidences (the verse of the Qur'ān and the above tradition) that will explain the entire meaning of *ribā* for us. Now, it is true that the *fuqahā'* use the term *nasā'* more often than the term *nasī'ah* when they are referring to delay in transactions identified by the *Sunnah*. They do use the term *nasī'ah* when they are talking about delay in transactions described by the Qur'ān. Yet, there is no difference between the two terms and both mean delay in a counter-value. Moreover, this separate use of the term is not absolute. The *fuqahā'* use the term interchangeably as well. We have quoted al-Jaṣṣāṣ above where he is using *nasā'* and *nasī'ah* for the same meaning. We have also quoted al-Sanhūrī to show his confusion when he cannot decide what to do with the term *nasī'ah* mentioned by the *Sunnah*.

Consequently, there is no justification whatsoever for separating the two terms and saying that *ribā al-nasī'ah* is *ribā* of

the Qur'ān and *ribā al-nasā'* is applied to delay in transactions in the *Sunnah*.

The term *nasī'ah* is used merely as an adjective to show that the transaction has a period of delay in it. It is in this sense that the term *bay' al-nasī'ah* is used to indicate a sale in which the price is delayed, which modern scholars have chosen to call *bay' bi-thaman ājil*, perhaps on the assumption that by using this term they can escape some of the rules of *fiqh*.

What then is the difference between the use of the term *ribā al-nasī'ah* by modern scholars and as used by the *fuqahā'*? Modern scholars use the term and mean a loan of money with interest. Thus, where A gives a loan of 100 *dīnārs* to B at 10% interest, this entire transaction is called *ribā al-nasī'ah* by modern scholars. The *fuqahā'* apply the term *ribā al-nasī'ah* (or *ribā al-nasā'*) to mean NOT the entire transaction, but *ribā* arising due to delay. **This is the same as the time value of money.** The exact details of their view will be absolutely clear in the following sections.

3.2 The term *bay'* means exchange of two counter-values. It has a very wide application. It is not confined to the term "sale of goods" as used in the law.

The word *bay'* is usually translated as sale and in this sense it is meant to signify what the term "sale of goods" signifies. The exchange or trade of currencies is not included in the term "sale of goods." The term *bay'*, on the other hand, means trade of all kinds where two counter-values are exchanged. In this sense, it is better to translate it as "exchange." In this meaning, *bay'* includes within it the meaning of *ṣarf*, which is the contract that deals with currencies and loans. The contract is treated as one category of *bay'* (exchange).

3.3 A loan is in reality nothing more than an exchange of currencies and in this sense it is included in the meaning of the term *ṣarf* and hence *bay'*.

If A gives $100 to B with the condition that he pay back $100 or even $120 after a year, he is actually selling $100 for $100 or $120 to be paid in the future. Those who cannot comprehend this simple concept, or do not wish to do so for some reason of their own, should stop reading this book for they will never understand the meaning of *ribā* as elaborated by the jurists. Another reason for including loans in *bay'* is to indicate that a loan that is given by way of *bay'* is a business transaction, while *qarḍ* is a charitable transaction and not a sale.

> The moment we consider a loan to be a sale of currency for currency with a delay, with or without excess in one counter-value, everything starts falling into place and the writings of the *fuqahā'* on the issue becomes absolutely clear.

3.4 Thus, when the *Sunnah* speaks of *ribā*, it is talking equally about loans as well as all other forms of interest, because a loan in reality is a sale of currency for currency with a delay.

It is, therefore, incorrect to say that the *Sunnah* deals with *ribā* in sales, while the Qur'ān deals with *ribā* in loans. Both sources talk about all forms of *ribā* including loans. Further, we consider the view of an economist that the *Sunnah* speaks of *ribā* to discourage barter to be misdirected. The powerful tradition mentioned by Jaṣṣāṣ holds the key to the meaning of all forms of *ribā*.

3.5 It is not correct to say that no definition of *ribā* has been provided. The jurists did provide definitions of *ribā* and all such definitions have the same meaning. Further, the definitions conform with the texts of the Qur'ān and the *Sunnah*.

The literal meaning of *ribā* is "excess." As already stated, this meaning was converted into a technical (*shar'ī*) meaning by the texts. The jurists define *ribā* in terms of this technical meaning.

A simple and short definition is given by by al-Sarkhsī in his book *al-Mabsūṭ*:

فأما الربا فى اللغة، هو الزيادة . . . و فى الشريعة الربا هو الفضل الخالى عن العوض المشروط فى البيع

The translation is:

> *Ribā* in its literal meaning is excess ...and in the technical sense (in the *sharī'ah*), *ribā* is the stipulated excess devoid of a (lawful) counter-value in *bay'* (sale).[22]

The first thing that strikes the reader in this and in any other definition of *ribā* provided by the *fuqahā'* is that it does not mention loans or debts. It clearly points out that *ribā* is relevant only in sales, that is, it is an excess stipulated in sales. What about loans? We have already explained that loans are included in the meaning of *bay'*, therefore, loans are included in this definition. We do not need to delve on the point further.

The main points in the definition provided by al-Sarakhsī are:

1. *Ribā* is excess.
2. It is an excess that is stipulated in a *bay'* (exchange).
3. It is an excess that is without a lawful counter-value.

22. Al-Sarakhsī, *al-Mabsūṭ*, vol. 12, 109.

Ribā is excess, nothing more nothing less. **This excess, however, is revealed in two ways: excess in quantity or amount and excess from the benefits of delay.** The word used in Arabic for delay is *nasī'ah* or *nasā'*. Thus, according to the jurists, there are two manifestations of the excess called *ribā*: excess through *qadr* (estimation) and excess through *nasī'ah* or *nasā'* (delay).

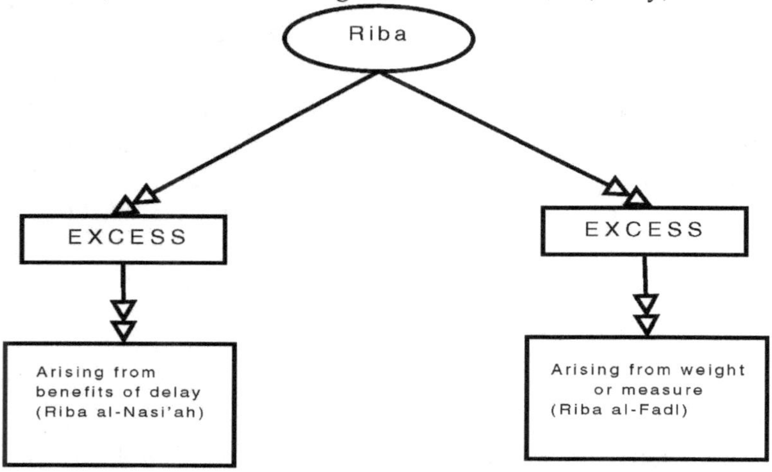

The first is the excess that is discovered by weighing, measuring, or counting the two quantities being exchanged in a *bay'*. If one of the parties has one hundred gold *dīnārs* in his hand, while the other party has one hundred and ten, the excess in the possession of the second party is ten, and this is revealed through counting. Likewise, if one party has hundred grams of gold, while the other has one hundred and ten grams, the excess is ten grams revealed through weighing. If the nature of the transaction being undertaken by the two parties is usurious according to the *sharī'ah*, this kind of excess is called *ribā al-faḍl* or excess revealed through weighing, measuring, or counting, that is, estimation (*qadr*).

If no excess is revealed on either side through weighing, counting, or measuring, that is, when the two items of exchange are exactly equal, there is yet a possibility of another kind of excess. This possibility is there even when an excess is found on the basis of weighing and so on. This takes place when one of the parties makes the payment or delivery at the time of the contract and it is stipulated that the other party will deliver an equal amount (or an amount in excess) after a period of one year; there is an excess in terms of the benefits that one party will enjoy during the period of one year. This is the party taking delivery and then making the delivery after one year, the party who uses, say, one hundred grams of gold for one year.

If this transaction falls under the provisions of *ribā*, it is called *ribā al-nasī'ah* or *ribā* arising from the utilisation of the commodity during the period of delay. The word *nasī'ah* is used by the *fuqahā'* in its literal meaning of delay. ***Ribā al-nasī'ah*, therefore, means *ribā* arising out of delay.** Likewise, if there is delay in a sale that is not usurious, they would call it *bay' al-nasī'ah*, which is the ordinary credit sale.

On the basis of these two kinds of excess, the jurists say that *ribā* consists of two kinds of excess: excess through *qadr* and excess of *nasī'ah*. It is for this reason that Ibn Rushd says:

> The jurists unanimously agreed about *ribā* in *bay'* that it is of two kinds: delayed (*nasī'ah*) and stipulated excess (*tafāḍul*).

Al-Sarakhsī explains the meaning of the two kinds of *ribā*, by elaborating the meaning of *faḍl*, as follows:

> [The words] "*faḍl* is *ribā*" imply *faḍl* through *qadr* and they imply *faḍl* through a period of delay, and both are intended. This was elaborated in the tradition of 'Ubādah ibn al-Ṣāmit, may Allāh be pleased with him.[23]

The tradition of 'Ubādah ibn al-Ṣāmit will be studied later for the whole meaning. For the present we may look at the comprehensive definition provided the great jurist Abū Bakr al-Kāsānī:

والكلام في مسائل الرّبا في الأصل في ثلاثة مواضع : أحدها في بيان الرّبا في عرف الشّرع أنّه ما هو، . . .

أمّا الأوّل فالرّبا في عرف الشّرع نوعان : ربا الفضل، وربا النّساء. أمّا ربا الفضل فهو : زيادة عين مال شرطت في عقد البيع على المعيار الشّرعيّ، وهو الكيل، أو الوزن في الجنس عندنا وعند الشّافعيّ هو : زيادة مطلقة في المطعوم خاصّة عند اتّحاد الجنس خاصّة. وأمّا ربا

23. Al-Sarakhsī, *al-Mabsūṭ*, vol 12, 111.

النّساء فهو فضل الحلول على الأجل، وفضل العين على الدّين في المكيلين، أو الموزونين عند اختلاف الجنس، أو في غير المكيلين، أو الموزونين عند اتّحاد الجنس عندنا وعند الشّافعيّ رحمه الله هو فضل الحلول على الأجل في المطعومات، والأثمان خاصّة، والله تعالى أعلم.

> The discussion about the issues of *ribā* is essentially on three points: First, about the elaboration of the meaning of *ribā* in the technical (legal) sense (*'urf shar'ī*), as to what it means. …
>
> *Ribā* in the jargon of the law (*'urf shar'ī*) is of two types: *ribā al-faḍl* and *ribā al-nasā'*. **As for *ribā al-faḍl,* it is the excess over the substance of the wealth that has been stipulated in the contract of *bay'* according to a legal criterion, which is [realized through] measure and weight in the genus,** while according to al-Shāfi'ī, it is the absolute excess specifically in food with uniformity of genus. **As for *ribā al-nasā'* it is the difference (excess) between the termination of delay and the period of delay and the difference (excess) between the possession (*'ayn*) and its non-possession (*dayn*) in things measured and weighed with different genera as well as in things measured and weighed with the uniformity of genera.** This is the meaning according to us (Ḥanafīs), and according to al-Shāfi'ī (God bless him), it is the difference between the termination of the period and the delay in foodstuffs and precious metals (with currency-value) specifically.[24]

What can be clearer than this? All that the present day reader has to keep in mind is that "loans" are included in the meaning of *bay'*.

Thus, the terms *ribā al-nasī'ah* or *ribā al-nasā'* are consistently applied by all the jurists to the type of *ribā* or excess that is revealed through delay. They do not say that this is the *ribā* of the Qur'ān or of the *Sunnah*; such a distinction does not exist for them.

Let us move a step further and make some vital distinctions between the two kinds of *ribā*.

There are two factors that distinguish *ribā al-faḍl* from *ribā al-nasī'ah*: the method of estimation and the identification of the beneficiary.

In both kinds of *ribā,* an excess is revealed. They differ only in the method of estimation of this excess. *Ribā al-faḍl* is determined

24. Al-Kāsānī, *Badā'i' al-Ṣanā'i'*, vol. 5, 183.

through measure, weight, or count, depending on the commodity involved, while *ribā al-nasī'ah* depends on the period of delay, that is, the period for which the borrowed amount or commodity is used by the borrower—a month, year, or whatever.

The question as to who derives the benefit from each type of *ribā* identifies the crucial difference. This distinction is ignored by modern scholars. **In a transaction of loan, it is the lender of money who gets the excess known as *ribā al-faḍl*. On the other hand, the benefit of *ribā al-nasī'ah* goes to the borrower, who uses the amount or commodity during the period of delay or repayment.**

We may now examine the sources to see how the *fuqahā'* understand them, and how the rules of *ribā* stated in this definition are linked directly to the texts.

CHAPTER 4

THE TEXTS OF *RIBĀ* INTERPRETED BY THE JURISTS

In the previous chapter, we saw that al-Jaṣṣāṣ maintains that the entire prohibition of *ribā* covering all *ribā*-bearing transactions are contained in two evidences: one is a text of the Qur'ān and the other is a tradition that elaborates the meaning in the Qur'ān.

4.1 The governing text of the Qur'ān contains an objection that is still repeated by those who argue against the prohibition of *ribā*.

ذٰلك بأنّهم قالوا إنّما البيع مثل الرّبٰو وأحلّ الله البيع و حرّم الرّبٰو

That is because they say: "Trade is like *ribā*," but Allah hath permitted trade and prohibited *ribā*.[25]

According to al-Jaṣṣāṣ, as we saw in the previous chapter, the controlling words are "and prohibited *ribā*." All forms of prohibited *ribā* are included in these words. The word *ribā*, he says, is in need of elaboration as it is *mujmal* (unelaborated) and such elaboration always comes from the *Sunnah*.

Before, we turn to the *Sunnah* for such an elaboration, we need to understand the statement "trade is like *ribā*." What kind of objection is this? What is this similarity between trade and *ribā* that is intended here? It is the same objection that is repeated again and again: "But interest is rent on capital," or "Interest is return on capital." Some go into details: "What is the difference between buying a house and consuming rent on it and putting money in a bank and consuming interest?" The statements can be multiplied. It is the same thing that the Jews are saying here: "But trade is like *ribā*?" In other words, there is nothing new in these objections. They were made fourteen centuries ago and have surely been around much before that. Let us understand the distinction between trade and *ribā* first.

25. Qur'ān 2 : 275. While we use the term "trade" for *bay'* following the acceptable translations, in reality it means "exchange is like *ribā*."

4.2 The distinction between trade and *ribā* is understood by comparing two apparently similar transactions, and both are forms of sale.

When scholars give explanations of the distinction, they might say that there is excessive profit in *ribā* and that is *ẓulm* (injustice), or that there is risk in trade and none in *ribā*. These are attempts to provide the underlying wisdom of the prohibition (the *ḥikmah*) and not the real distinction. It is the same as presenting a large number of economic theories that indicate the evils of *ribā*. These explanations may or may not be true, yet they do not constitute legal reasoning. The jurist is interested in the legal rule as it relates to the distinction. It is the legal rule that will tell him about the nature of the prohibition. We will turn to the wisdom of the prohibition later.

The distinction lies in comparing two credit sales. As both are credit sales, with one being prohibited and the other permitted, the comparison has real meaning for us. Now it is well known that when a person sells on cash he charges less, but when he gives the buyer a credit for a stipulated period he charges a little more depending on the extent of the delay. As a general rule (without going into details here) the sale of goods on credit with an enhanced price is permitted in Islamic law, and it was permitted at the time the objection was raised.

Let us consider two transactions "X" and "Z." In transaction "X," the seller A sells to the buyer B 100 gold *dīnārs*, with a delay of one year, for 110 *dīnārs*. We have called this transaction a sale, but it can be seen very easily that this is a loan transaction. One person has given a loan to another for one year at 10% interest. **It is important to remember that for the analysis of *ribā* in Islamic law, a loan or debt will always be treated as a sale transaction.** In practice, it does not matter and we may look at it as a loan transaction; the nature of the underlying transaction does not change whatever we call it.

In "Z," the second transaction, A is selling 100 bags of wheat to B, by giving him credit of one year, for a sum of 110 *dīnārs*. We may assume here that had the buyer paid cash on the spot, the 100 bags of wheat would have cost him 100 *dīnārs*. He is charging an extra 10 for the delay of one year. It is also obvious that in transaction "X" had the seller demanded exactly similar *dīnārs* for his 100, the buyer would not have given him more than 100 *dīnārs*.

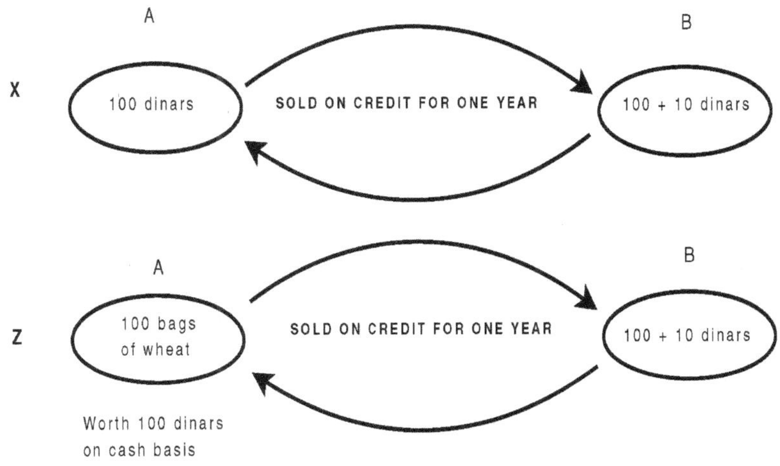

In Islamic law, transaction "X" is prohibited, while transaction "Z" is permitted. This is quite confusing for the persons raising the objection. They would say, "Transaction X is just like transaction Z insofar as an extra 10 is being charged for delay in both transactions that are of equal value." In other words, they are saying, "Trade is like *ribā*." The response is quite clear. In our words, "Allāh has permitted transaction Z and prohibited transaction X." In the words of the Qur'ān, "Allah has permitted trade and prohibited *ribā*."

4.3 *Ribā* is a matter of ritual obedience for we do not know the underlying reason for the prohibition.

At once the question arises in the mind, "But why has Allah prohibited transaction X?" Using our rational faculty, we can come up with numerous reasons: so that wealth does not circulate among the rich alone (spoils of war), that is, distributive justice; so that there is no *ẓulm* (injustice); so that profit is based on risk and not on a guaranteed return. All of these may be the correct reasons and yet we can never be sure. It is Allāh alone who knows. In other words, the prohibition of *ribā* is a matter of ritual obedience. It is *ta'abbudī*. It is prohibited because Allāh Almighty has said it is prohibited. It is the law. Violating the command means facing a declaration of war from Allāh and his Messenger (pbuh).

4.4 The information we have inferred from the verse so far is about a single transaction. We need more information; we need to know about all the transactions that are prohibited.

Transaction X in the previous section gives us a rule that the loan transaction with interest is prohibited. The verse of the Qur'ān,

و أحلّ الله البيع و حرّم الرّبا

And Allāh has permitted sale and prohibited (*ribā*).

however, gives us a general principle, according to al-Jaṣṣāṣ, who maintains that all forms of *ribā* are prohited by this verse. This means that it is a broad general principle that governs a large number of rules. How do we derive these rules? How do we come to know of all the transactions covered by the principle? To do so, we move to the next evidence mentioned by al-Jaṣṣāṣ.

4.5 The tradition of 'Ubādah ibn al-Ṣāmit (God be pleased with him) determines the rules of *ribā* and elaborates the general principle in the Qur'ān.

وعن عبادة بن الصّامت قال : قال رسول الله صلّى الله عليه وسلّم عّالذّهب بالذّهب، والفضّة بالفضّة، والبرّ بالبرّ، والشّعير بالشّعير، والتّمر بالتّمر، والملح بالملح، مثلا بمثل، سواءا بسواء، يدا بيد، فإذا اختلف هٰذه الأصناف فبيعوا كيف شئتم إذا كان يدا بيدٌ رواه مسلم.

> From 'Ubādah ibn al-Ṣāmit, who said, "The Messenger of Allāh (God's peace and blessings be upon him) said, 'Gold for gold, silver for silver, wheat for wheat, barley for barley, dates for dates, salt for salt, like for like, in equal weights, and from hand to hand. If these species differ, then, sell as

> you like, as long as it is from hand to hand.' " It is reported by Muslim.[26]

A tradition very similar to this from Abū Sa'īd al-Khudrī(God be pleased with him) was used by Muḥammad al-Shaybānī, the disciple of Abū Ḥanīfah, in the beginning of three separate books of law. These were the book of sales and *salam*, the book of *ṣarf*, and the book of *ijārah*. Al-Sarakshsī points this out as follows:

> Muḥammad commenced the book of sales with a part of it, as he did the book of hire and the book of *ṣarf*, and a tradition like it is a valid legal evidence with which laws in addition to those in the Qur'ān can be laid down.[27]

This tradition, that is the one from 'Ubādah ibn al-Ṣāmit (God be pleased with him), controls the meaning of *ribā* in Islamic law. It gives a full elaboration of the meaning of the term *ribā* as used in the Qur'ān. Yet it has continued to perplex many modern *fiqh* scholars and economists alike. Some economists think that is is meant to discourage barter and encourage trading in currencies. *Fiqh* scholars think that it deals with some kind of *ribā* that is trivial. Others call it *ribā* of sales or simply *ribā al-faḍl*. We are sorry to say that all these interpretations are not sound. The reason may be that it sounds quite confusing as to why one person should pick up his 100 *dīnārs* from home, go to the market and exchange them with *dīnārs* of the same number and return home, or his bag of wheat for a similar bag of wheat of equal weight.

Yet, the earlier jurists have never been confused about the meaning of this tradition. They have seen its clear instructions and implemented its rules with great precision. They treat it as an elaboration of the meaning of *ribā* in the Qur'ān and as a basis for identifying all *ribā*-bearing transactions including loans.

26. Al-Ṣan'ānī, *Subul al-Salām Sharḥ Bulūgh al-Marām*, vol. 3, 72.
27. Al-Sarakhsī, *al-Mabsūṭ*, vol. 12, 110.

4.6 The tradition of 'Ubādah ibn al-Ṣāmit (God be pleased with him), however, is either misinterpreted by modern scholars or the statements of the earlier jurists elaborating its meaning are intentionally ignored.

What is a matter of amazement for us is why modern scholars do not understand this tradition, the way the jurists have understood it, and continue to attribute interpretations to it that are either meaningless or completely misdirected? A cause of further surprise is when these scholars ignore clear statements made by jurists and continue with interpretations they have set their minds on. Is this intentional? There is no way of knowing.

By way of illustration, we refer to Mawlana Taqi Usmani, who is considered a leading and respected scholar. To elaborate a point in the judgement on *ribā*, the learned scholar quotes al-Ghazālī in detail. The same or a similar quotation is produced on some web sites as well. Yet, the scholar avoids or does not mention a clear statement by al-Ghazālī that explains the true meaning of the tradition as well as the nature of loans in Islam. He could not have missed this statement for he refers to the rest of al-Ghazālī's text by way of explanation. The quotations we give below are lengthy, yet they are extremely important to understand the meaning of the tradition and to analyse the approach of modern scholars. We first reproduce the translation provided by Mawlana Taqi Usmani in the judgement on *ribā*, and then follow it up with the text that he ignores. Imām al-Ghazālī's text reproduced by Taqi Usmani is as follows:

> The creation of dirhams and dinars (money) is one of the blessings of Allah. They are stones having no intrinsic usufruct or utility, but all human beings need them, because every body needs a large number of commodities for his eating, wearing etc, and often he does not have what he needs and does have what he needs not, therefore, the transactions of exchange are inevitable. But there must be a measure on the basis of which price can be determined, because the exchanged commodities are neither of the same type, nor of the same measure which can determine how much quantity of one commodity is a just price for another.

Therefore, all these commodities need a mediator to judge their exact value. Allah Almighty has, therefore, created dirhams and dinars (money) as judges and mediators between all commodities so that all objects of wealth are measured through them and their being the measure of the value of all commodities is based on the fact that they are not an objective in themselves. Had they been an objective in themselves, one could have a specific purpose for keeping them which might have given them more importance according to his intention while the one who had no such purpose would have not given them such importance and thus the whole system would have been disturbed. That is why Allah has created them, so that they may be circulated between hands and act as a fair judge between different commodities and work as a medium to acquire other things. So, the one who owns them is as he owns every thing, unlike the one who owns a cloth, because he owns only a cloth, therefore, if he needs food, the owner of the food may not be interested in exchanging his food for cloth, because he may need an animal for example. Therefore, there was needed a thing which in its appearance is nothing, but in its essence is everything. The thing which has no particular form may have different forms in relation to other things like a mirror which has no color, but it reflects every colour. The same is the case of money. It is not an objective in itself, but it is an instrument to lead to all objectives. So, the one who is using money in a manner contrary to its basic purpose is, in fact, disregarding the blessings of Allah. Consequently, whoever hoards money is doing injustice to it and is defeating their actual purpose. He is like the one who detains a ruler in a prison. And whoever effects the transactions of interest on money is, in fact, discarding the blessing of Allah and is committing injustice, because money is created for some other things, not for itself. So, the one who has started trading in money itself has made it an objective contrary to the original wisdom behind its creation, because it is injustice to use money for a purpose other than it was created for. If it is allowed for him to trade in money itself, money will become his ultimate goal and will remain detained with him like hoarded money. And imprisoning a ruler or restricting a postman from conveying messages is nothing but injustice.[28]

There is no doubt that this is an outstanding passage about the nature of currency and the prohibition of transactions in this ultimate commodity. We wonder, however, why Mawlāna Taqi Usmani did not translate the next paragraph? Perhaps, responsibility has been evaded in a subtle way through a statement in the footnote that we have rendered in bold. It may be noted that the statement in the footnote "He has further discussed that the impermissibility of trading in money is applicable to the units of the same denomination," shows that Taqi Usmani has read the passage and is fully aware of it, yet he does not give it effect in his understanding of the issue.

The pargraph following these words contains a crucial statement that contains the key to the understanding of the tradition of Ubādah ibn al-Ṣāmit. The Imām raises a question: If someone asks, if it is true that transactions in the identical currencies are not intended then why has the sale of one *dirham* for an identical *dirham* been permitted, as in the traditions similar to the one narrated by 'Ubādah ibn al-Ṣāmit?

28. The note appended to the text in the judgement says: "This is an abridged translation of the detailed discussion of Imam Al-Ghazali in his landmark work 'Ihya-al-Uloom' V.4, P. 88-89, Cairo 1939. **He has further discussed that the impermissibility of trading in money is applicable to the units of the same denomination. However, exchange of different currencies is allowed. He has also explained the difference between these two situations."**

4.7 Imām al-Ghazālī clearly states that *qarḍ*, if it is not *qarḍ ḥasan* given out of compassion, is prohibited and amounts to *ẓulm*; further, the exchange of a *dirham* for a *dirham* (on spot basis) gives rise to a meaningless transaction for the tradition of 'Ubādah ibn al-Ṣāmit (God be pleased with him) and others are in reality elaborating rules.

The Imām proceeds to answer the question he raises and unravels the key to the understanding of these traditions. Imām al-Ghazālī (God bless him) continues (the crucial sentences are in bold):

> ...just like his confinement is injustice. Consequently, the sale of currency for currency has no meaning except the acquisition of currency for hoarding, which is injustice. **If you say: Why has the sale of one currency been permitted for another, and why has the sale of a *dirham* been permitted for another *dirham* (on spot basis)?** Know then that one (minted) currency may differ from another with respect to the objective of acquiring other things, for acquisition may be facilitated by one of the two due to its excess. It is just like *dirhams* that differ so very slightly from each other. Thus, preventing their exchange will frustrate the purpose that is specific to them, which is the facility of reaching other things through it. **As for the sale of a *dirham* with an identical *dirham*, it is permitted because no rational person will desire it as long as they are equivalent and no trader will undertake this transaction. It is similar to the act of putting the *dirhams* on the ground and picking up the same *dirhams*. We have no fear that reasonable persons will employ their time in placing their *dirhams* on the ground and picking them up. We, therefore, do not prohibit something that is not desired by the persons. Unless, one is of a better quality than the other, but this too cannot be conceived in practice. The reason is that the owner of good quality will not agree to exchange**

> **it for identical quantities of bad quality. The contract is thus not established....**
>
> **If, however, he sells a *dirham* for an identical *dirham* with a delay, then this is not permitted for he has not offered this to the other by way of permission (of use) intending *iḥsān* through *qarḍ*, which is generosity and a praiseworthy act on his part and it is a form of transaction that yields praise and (spiritual) reward for the person giving the permission. Offering it in a manner that brings no praise nor (spiritual) reward also amounts to injustice for it loses the merit of permission (of use) and turns it into a commutative transaction.**

The illustrious Imām is making the following points:

1. If *dirhams* of different qualities are exchanged, then, this makes some sense and sale is possible. Later in the passage he goes to show that even this is not allowed for the same currency (for reasons of *ribā*) with a difference and the two sides, good quality and bad quality, have to be made equal.

2. That, in a spot transaction, no sane person will exchange a number of *dirhams* with *dirhams* in the same number and of an identical type. This will amount to putting the money on the ground and picking it up. Even Imām al-Sarakhsī says something similar: "The reason is that delivering a thing for its own genus deprives the contract of any utility, with one thing being both the payment and the commodity delivered along with an excess that is devoid of compensation...."

3. That, in a spot transaction, no one will exchange a number of good quality *dirhams* for the same number of bad quality *dirhams*, as this would entail a manifest loss for one person.

4. The last paragraph is extremely important. He says that if one *dirham* is exchanged for an identical *dirham* **with a delay** then this is a *qarḍ* transaction. **This is a *qarḍ* transaction that is not the *qarḍ* that we call *qarḍ ḥasan*, therefore, it is prohibited for it is *ẓulm*.**

In short, he is saying that this tradition is not meant to give permission to transactions rather it is a tradition that elaborates the rules of *ribā*. This is a Shāfi'ī jurist attempting to explain the meaning of the tradition. The position is the same in all schools. The only difference is that in some cases the elaboration provided is in detail, while in other texts it is assumed that the reader understands the obvious meaning. Why then do modern Muslim scholars ignore the meaning given to the traditions by the earlier jurists? Why did Taqi Usmani ignore the very important statement about the prohibition of a *qarḍ* that is not a *qarḍ ḥasan*. The answer will be obvious when we understand the meaning and full impact of the tradition.

> The main question that arises here is: We now know that *ribā* is prohibited, but from the statement of Imām al-Ghazālī above we understand that a business loan, that is not given to the borrower as a *qard ḥasan*, is also prohibted? Why is such a loan prohibited? What is the evidence for this ruling?

In the next section, we will explain the rules emerging from the tradition by relying on the text of the great Ḥanafī jurist al-Sarakhsī.

4.8 The tradition of 'Ubādah (God be pleased with him) is not saying that you undertake the transactions mentioned; it is saying that if you undertake such transactions, then, here are the rules you must follow.

As Imām al-Ghazālī has explained, no one is going to pick up his 100 dinars and exchange them on a spot basis for similar 100 dinars of another person, nor is he going to pay 110 dinars for 100 dinars of the other person. Yes, when the transactions involve deffered payments, there may be a desire on the part of the parties to make such exchanges. That is where the rules come in. The rules are contained in the tradition under examination. We will borrow the explanation from Imām al-Sarakhsī. He says:

> This is a *mashhūr* tradition that has been readily accepted by the jurists, may Allāh have mercy on them. Because of its being practiced and because of its being well-known, Muḥammad commenced the book of sales with a part of it, as he did the book of hire and the book of *ṣarf*, and a tradition like it is a valid legal evidence with which laws in addition to those in the Qur'ān can be laid down, in our view (Ḥanafī view). The tradition has been reported by four

> Companions, may Allāh be pleased with them all, with a slight difference in the words: 'Umar ibn al-Khaṭṭāb, 'Ubādah ibn al-Ṣāmit, Abū Sa'īd al-Khudrī, and Mu'āwiyah ibn Abī Sufyān, may Allāh be pleased with them all.
>
> The tradition includes the *tafsīr* (commentary), the *ḥukm*, and the rules related to the *ḥukm* in its sub-issues.

After this, the Imām goes into the *tafsīr* elaborating the meaning of each individual word or phrase. We have translated this elsewhere so we are not going to reproduce the whole text. This is followed by the *ḥukm* contained in the tradition, that is, the rules to be followed. He says the following:

> As for the *ḥukm*, the tradition contains two of them (*ḥukmān*):
>
> 1. the prohibition of *nasā'* (delay) in these commodities during exchange in the same species, which is agreed upon;
> 2. and, the prohibition of *tafāḍul*, which is the opinion of the majority of the Companions, may Allāh be pleased with them.

The elaboration of the rules follows in a large number of cases laid down by Imām Abū Ḥanīfah and his illustrious companions. As it is important to understand the rules in their totality, we shall devote the next chapter to the elaboration of these rules as found in books of *fiqh*, in particular *al-Mabsūṭ* by Imām al-Sarakhsī.

CHAPTER 5

THE RULES OF PROHIBITION OF *RIBĀ* EMERGING FROM THE *SUNNAH*

5.1 The nature of rules in Islamic law is understood through the terms *'aẓīmah* (initial broad rule) and *rukhṣah* (exemption).

These are terms that are used in *uṣūl al-fiqh* to indicate the analytical and consistent structure of the law. The term *'azīmah* (lit. determination, resolution) is applied to mean a rule that is applied initially and for itself. Such rules form the backbone of the law. As against this, there may be a rule that goes contrary to the requirements of the initial rule, but is permitted by the law. This rule is considered to be a *rukhṣah* (exemption) from the initial rule. Thus, many people fail to understand why we say, for example, that the contract of *salam* (advance payment) is considered a *rukhṣah*. The reason is that they are looking at the exempted case and not at the initial rule.

The benefit of this structure is that it explains why two opposing cases may be permitted by the law. **Further, it is not permitted to extend the exemption through analogy, while the initial rule can be extended in this way. A jurist must always be aware of the *'azā'im* and *rukhaṣ* of the law.** Some jurists like al-Qarāfī have maintained that this structure prevails throughout the entire law.

This point has been mentioned here because it is of great significance in the topic of *ribā*. The reason is that the jurists are not allowed to build up an entire legal sub-system on the basis of exemptions. This would amount to the negation of the broad primary provisions of the law. Thus, if bankers and economists today attempt to create new forms of banking transactions all of which are created upon *rukhas* (exemptions) it would not be permitted as the prohibition of *ribā* will be reduced to a farce. The only exemptions allowed are those mentioned in the texts. The questions that economists will be asked are: Is *salam* an exemption? Is *murābaḥa* an exemption? Is *muḍārabah* an exemption? Such questions will ensure the erection of the economic system on sound lines from the Islamic point of view.

5.2 The structure of general rules and exemptions is nowhere more obvious than in the issue of *ribā*.

The Qur'ān lays down a broad general principle about the prohibition of *ribā*: "Allah has permitted exchange and prohibited *ribā*." We have already discussed this principle at length. The general principle contains within it a number of rules that identify the cases of *ribā* and determine their nature. The rules are followed by exemptions that the *sharī'ah* has provided. According to the discipline of *uṣūl al-fiqh*, the exemptions are limited to the permission granted and cannot be extended to apply to new cases.

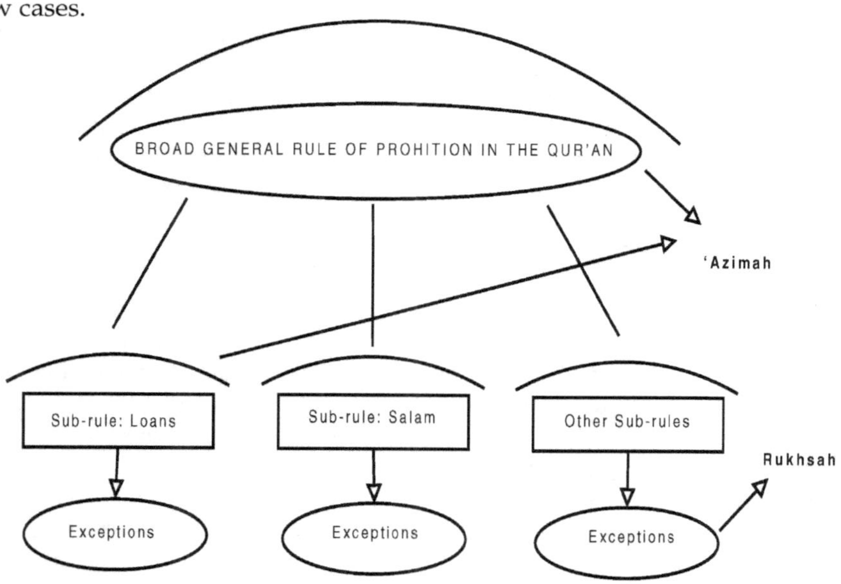

At the end of the previous chapter, we noted that the tradition of 'Ubādah ibn al-Ṣāmit (R) contains two *aḥkām*. We will see the impact of these *aḥkām* now and derive the rules pertaining to *ribā*.

5.3 The first set of rules tell us that all loans, with or without interest are prohibited; the only loan permitted is the *qarḍ ḥasan,* which is a charitable not a business transaction.

The tradition of 'Ubādah ibn al-Ṣāmit contains commands that have to be complied with individually and also together wherever possible. Let us list these commands; they can be divided into two groups, however, we must have a transaction to which these rules apply:

We begin with the loan transaction, or the sale of gold dinars for gold dinars with an excess, in which A has 100 gold dinars that he is about to give to B with the stipulation that B will pay 100 dinars plus 10 dinars after one year.

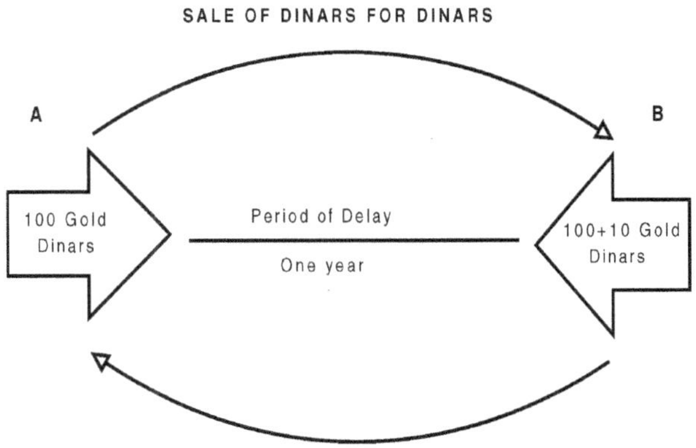

Now the commands in the tradition are:

Group 1 Dealing in the same species (Gold for Gold, say)

a) Make the weights equal on both sides.
b) Exchange the two commodities immediately.

Group 2 Dealing in the same species (Gold for Siver, say)

1. There is no harm if the two counter-values are unequal.
2. But exchange immediately.

The transaction is that of group 1, therefore, the first command in the tradition says to A and B: ***Make the two counter-values equal.*** When the parties comply with the command, the remaining transaction is as follows:

The transaction is still that of group 1, therefore, the second command in the tradition says to A and B: ***Exchange the two counter-values at once.*** When the parties comply with the command, the remaining transaction is what has been described by Imām al-Ghazāli as "**putting your dinars on the ground and picking them up.**" No one is interested in undertaking this transaction and neither is the tradition; it is merely laying down the rules.

SALE OF DINARS FOR DINARS

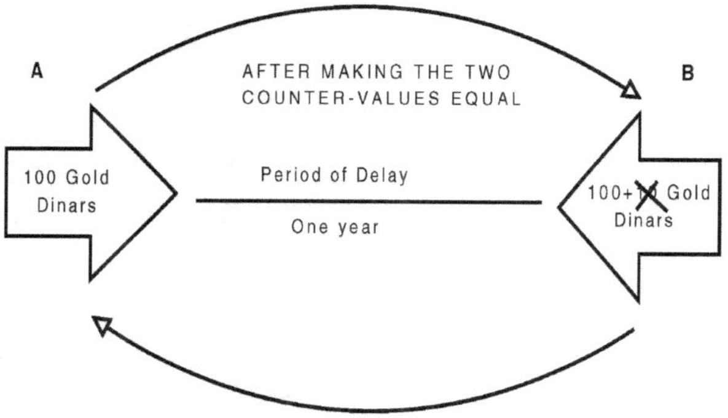

The combined impact of the command is:

> DO NOT SELL GOLD FOR GOLD, UNLESS THE WEIGHT ON BOTH SIDES IS EQUAL, AND UNLESS YOU EXCHANGE FROM HAND TO HAND.

The commands of the tradition, thus, prohibit this loan transaction or the sale of gold for gold with an excess and a period of delay. It can be seen that the same prohibition would apply even when the commodity exchanged is silver on both sides, or when minted gold coins are used. The illustration for an exchange of gold dinars for silver may be as follows:

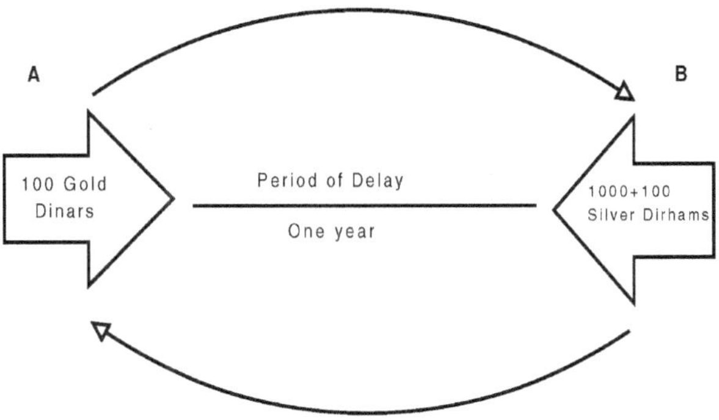

Here the transaction is that of group 2, therefore, the first command in the tradition says to A and B: ***There is no harm if the two counter-values are unequal.*** The second command in the tradition says to A and B: ***Exchange the two counter-values at once.*** This transaction is one that serves a need of the people and it is the exchange of one currency for another. The rate is whatever prevails in the market and is acceptable to the people. The same transaction with the a delay is not allowed as that may convert it into a loan with interest.

Before we proceed further, it is necessary to point out that in the transaction where 100 dinars of gold are to be exchanged for 110 dinars of gold with a delay of one year, both *faḍl* and *nasī'ah* are prohibited. The first command in group 1 prohibits *faḍl*, while the second command in the same group prohibits *nasī'ah*. In the transaction where dinars are exchanged for silver, *faḍl* is allowed, but *nasī'ah* is prohibited. This shows that *faḍl* and *nasī'ah* are not separate forms of *ribā*, but counter-values. In fact, *faḍl* is a counter-value for *nasī'ah*. Thus, saying that *nasī'ah* is *ribā* of the Qur'ān and *faḍl* is the *ribā* of the *Sunnah* is meaningless.

We are now ready to derive rules from the above transactions, and we will derive three rules. The first rule or sub-principle laid down by the tradition is:

Rule 1: The loan transaction with a stipulated excess in terms of amount and period of delay is prohibited.

This rule is derived from the combined impact of the two commands in group 1, as explained above. It is also derived from the impact of the second command in group 2, where gold is exchanged for silver.

Now the alert reader will notice that after the first command in group one is applied, the transaction we are left with is an interest-free loan. In other words, 100 dinars are to be exchanged with 100 dinars with a delay of one year. Nevertheless, the tradition says that there is no *faḍl* here, but one party is going to benefit without compensation by using the other person's dinars for one year, and this is *ribā al-nasī'ah*. The parties are required to exchange the two counter-values at once. We, therefore, have another rule.

Rule 2: An interest-free loan with a fixed period of repayment, given by way of business, is prohibited.

This may sound shocking to some, but it is true. Let us state the exception to rule 2, so that the shock is reduced:

Exception to Rule 2: An interest-free loan in which the period of use is donated by one party to the other party intending *iḥsān* through *qarḍ* is permitted and recommended, but such a loan cannot have a fixed period of repayment.

The conclusion is that only *qarḍ ḥasan* or a charitable loan is allowed in the manner recommended by the *sharī'ah* as it brings spiritual reward. An interest-free loan with a fixed period period of payment, given by way of business is not permitted. The broad and simple rule we may derive is: ***Business loans in any form, with or without interest, are not permitted in Islamic law.***

The third rule is derived from the transaction of gold with silver, or *dīnārs* and *dirhams*. The tradition does not permit a delay, because permitting delay amounts to permitting loan transactions.

Rule 3: When the species are different, unequal quantities can be exchanged, as long as the exchange is immediate, otherwise they will amount to loans with or without interest, and such loans are prohibited.

5.4 The credit sale is permitted as the methods of estimation, or the *sharī'ah* standard, is different.

When we look at the six commodities and try to apply the rules, it appears in the first instance that the credit sale (*bay' al-nasī'ah*) should be prohibited too. For example, if A is giving 10 *dīnārs* to B for 100 bags of wheat to be delivered after one year, the species are different, so 10 *dīnārs* can be paid for 100 bags of wheat, but the exchange has to be immediate according to rule 3. In other words, there should be no delay, which is the basis of the *bay' al-nasī'ah* or the credit-sale.

SELLING WHEAT ON CREDIT FOR DINARS

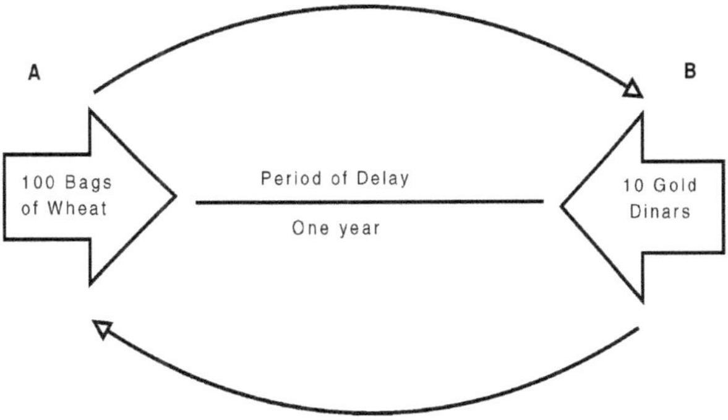

In the figure above, if rule 3 is applied, the credit sale will not be possible. The answer of the *fuqahā'* to this objection would be "no," the exchange does not have to be immediate. To understand this we have to comprehend the system used by the *fuqahā'* for determining the underlying causes, that is, the *'ilal*. Here we may simplify the issue by saying that if the method of estimation (*qadr*) is the same for the species, they have to be exchanged immediately, but when the method of estimation is different, delay is permitted. Thus, the method of estimating gold and silver is the same, therefore, these have to be exchanged at once. Wheat, however, has a different method of estimation; it is measured in containers or cubits. A system of measure was used for food items during the period of the Prophet (pbuh) and that is maintained by the *fuqahā'* for purpose of analysis. It is possible for A to pay 10 *dīnārs*, after one year, for 100 bags of wheat or barley or anything that is measured or counted, and take delivery of the wheat immediately. In other words, credit sale is allowed in such cases.

In fact, gold dinars and wheat are not even different species; they are different genera altogether. The Mālikī and Shāfi'ī jurists divide them into things with currency value and food. What about buying platinum or iron ore on credit by paying gold. Here too the jurists state that the method of weighing gold and silver is quite different from weighing iron ore. We have discussed this in detail elsewhere.[29] The jurists divide com-

29. See Imran Ahsan Khan Nyazee, *The Concept of Ribā*, chap. 6.

modities into different genera or categories, and credit sale is possible across these categories. The figure below elaborates this classification.

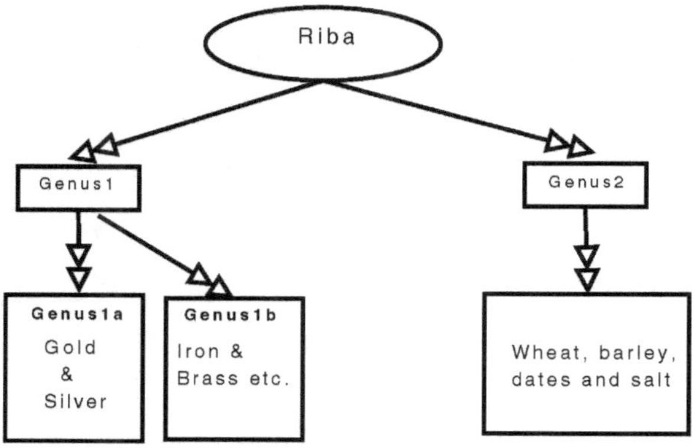

The above figure implies that metals can be sold on credit for currency, just as food can be sold on credit for currency. We, therefore, derive another rule:

Rule 4: When the genera or species are different and their method of estimation is different, unequal quantities can be exchanged even with a delay.

5.5 The prohibition of *ribā* affects the *salam* transaction as well, and it is permitted as an exemption (*rukhṣah*), therefore, it cannot be used for extending the rule to new forms of transactions.

The contract of *salam* is the opposite of the credit sale. It means making an advance payment for goods. In the context of the six commodities mentioned in the tradition, we have the following restrictive rule:

Rule 5: The contract of *salam* cannot be undertaken in currencies, as making advance payment for a currency with another currency will amount to a loan, with or without interest, and both are prohibited.

Thus, if A pays 100 dinars to B for 100 or 110 dinars of gold, or for 1000 or 1100 silver dirhams, with a delivery period of one year, the transaction is not valid, because this is the same loan transaction that is prohibited by Rules 1 to 3 above. There is no exception to this rule. **Thus, *salam* is not allowed in currencies.** This corollary emphasises that the interest free business loan, and obviously a loan with interest, is not permitted.

Salam is not allowed in currencies in another meaning as well. What if A wants to give 100 pounds of dates today for 20 *dīnārs* to be delivered after six months or a year. According to the jurists, this contract is not allowed either. There are some jurists who argue that this is in reality a credit-sale. Yet, those who disallow it maintain that currencies cannot be a commodity in this contract. This is a difficult debate. *Salam*, however, is an exemption from the impact of the tradition that says: "Do not sell what you do not have." It has been declared an exemption due to the need of the poor people. It is a basic rule that the permission granted by way of exemption cannot be extended by way of analogy or other rational means to permit new transactions.

5.6 The prohibition of *ribā* affects many other contracts.

5.7 Most of the above rules are supported by traditions other than that of 'Ubādah ibn al-Ṣāmit.

Most of the above rules, especially the classifications into different genera and species, are supported by traditions, and the *fuqahā'* use them to refine the concepts. For example, after a thorough examination of the above rules, the famous jurist Ibrāhīm al-Nakha'ī framed the following statement:

محمّد عن أبى حنيفة عن حمّاد عن ابراهيم أنّه قال: وأسلم ما يكال فيما يوزن وأسلم ما يوزن فيما يكال ولا تسلم ما يوزن فيما يوزن ولا ما يكال فيما يكال . واذا اختلف النوعان فيما لا يكال ولا يوزن فلا بأس به اثنان بواحد يد بيد ولا بأس به نسيئة .

> Muḥammad from Abū Ḥanīfah from Ḥammād from Ibrāhīm, who said: Exchange (make an advance payment with) what is measured for what is weighed, and an advance payment with what is weighed for what is measured,

> but do not make an advance payment with what is weighed for what is weighed nor with what is measured for what is measured. If the species are different in what is not measured or weighed then there is no harm in (exchanging) it, two for one, from hand to hand, and there is no harm in it (even) with a delay.

We have given the following figure to indicate this.

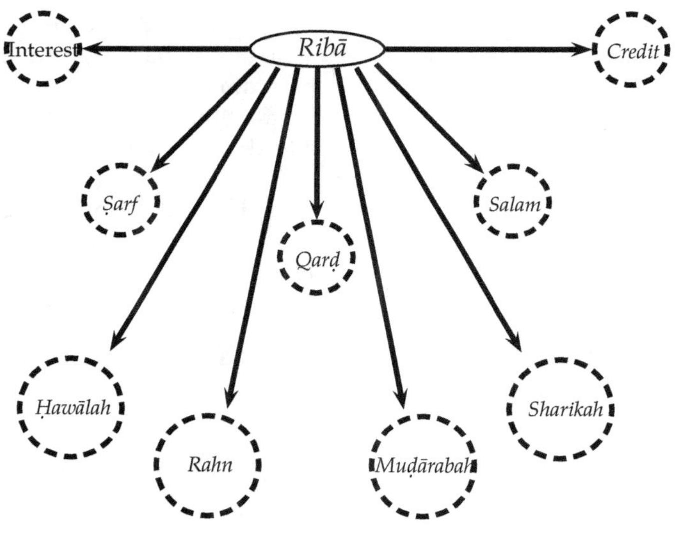

5.8 All the rules listed in the previous chapter and the current chapter were used to design or alter basic contracts, and the most important with respect to financial transactions was the contract of *ṣarf*.

It is a matter of great surprise that most modern scholars believe that the jurists did not talk about the loan transaction, and the rules for this vital transaction are to be derived directly from the Qur'ān. Nothing could be farther than the truth. The jurists applied the rules of *ribā* to many contracts, as indicated in the figure above. There is, however, one category of contracts that is governed entirely by the rules mentioned above. This was the contract of *ṣarf*. We shall now turn to a brief description of this contract so that the reader can see how the rules mentioned above are applied. In doing so, we shall point out the contradictions in the standards made for Islamic banking. These contradictions exist, because modern scholars who make rules for Islamic banking have ignored the writings of the jurists.

CHAPTER 6

ṢARF, QARḌ ḤASAN AND CONTRADICTIONS IN MODERN RULINGS

6.1 The contract of *ṣarf* is a kind of *bay'* with all kinds of currency transactions whether these are transactions in the same currency or the exchange of one currency with another.

The meaning of the contract of *ṣarf* is important to understand. The best definition is given by al-Kāsānī. He first says that among the types of *bay'* is the *ṣarf* contract, **which is exchange of *dayn* for *dayn*.** The term *dayn* is usuall translated as debt, but here it means currencies. The reason is that *dayn* is something that is established as a liability (against the *dhimmah*). In contracts, currency is something that is established against the *dhimmah*, that is, the party owes the amount just by referring to it. It is for this reason that al-Kāsānī says: "Whether it is an exchange of *dayn* for *dayn*, which is *dirhams* and *dīnārs*...."[30] We have explained all this in detail elsewhere.[31] By way of help, a detailed diagram explaining sales is given below:

Al-Kasānī then defines *ṣarf* as follows:

> *Ṣarf* in the technical understanding of the law is the name for the sale of absolute prices (currencies) one with the other. **It is the sale of gold (*dīnārs*) for gold (*dīnārs*), the sale of silver (*dirhams*) for silver (*dirhams*), and also the sale of one species (currency) with another.** This type of sale has been called *ṣarf* due to the meaning of return and transfer, just as it is said, "I transferred it from here to there." Likewise, it has been called *ṣarf* due to its exclusive application to the return of the counter-value and its transfer from

30. Al-Kāsānī, *Badā'i' al-Sanā'i'*, vol. 5, 455.
31. Imran A. Nyazee, *The Concept of Ribā* 2d ed. (Islamabad: Advanced Legal Studies Institute, 2008), 64.

hand to hand (immediately). It is also probable that it has been called *ṣarf* due to the meaning of excess (*tafāḍul*).[32]

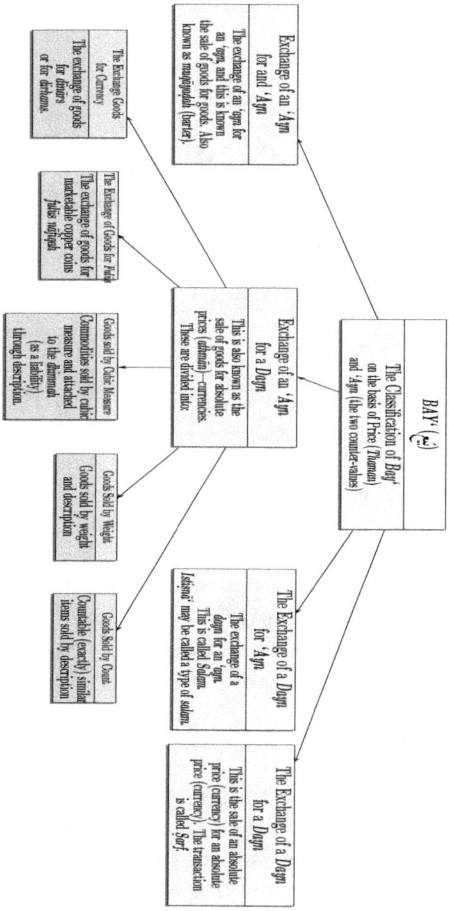

This definition clearly states that the contract applies to the sale of a currency for itself. This is the meaning of the sale of *dīnārs* for *dīnārs* and the sale of *dirhams* for *dirhams*. We have highlighted this meaning in the definition. It may be mentioned here that when gold and silver are

32. Al-Kāsānī, *Badā'i' al-Sanā'i'*, vol. 5, 453.

mentioned in traditions, the jurists usually take the meaning to be *dīnārs* and *dirhams*.

There is no harm in repeating here what we have said above that the sale of a currency for itself, when one counter-value is delayed, amounts to a loan. Thus, the contract of *ṣarf* applies to loan transactions.

The contract also applies to the exchange of one currency with another currency, like *dīnārs* for *dirhams*. If there is a delay in such a transaction, this too can be converted into a loan.

6.2 The evidence for the validity of *ṣarf* is a tradition from 'Abd Allāh ibn 'Umar (R), while the tradition from 'Ubādah (R) lays down its rules.

The Shari'ah Standard on trading in currencies issued by AOIFI says that the evidence for the legal validity of *ṣarf* is the tradition of 'Ubādah ibn al-Ṣāmit (God be pleased with him) that we have discussed above. We have to disagree with them on this count. This tradition gives us the rules for *ṣarf* and for transactions involving *ribā*. We disagree with them, because the jurists disagree with them. Does it matter? Yes, it does as an institution attempting to direct Islamic banking should be precise and not sloppy. The evidence for the validity of *ṣarf*, according to the earlier jurists, is as follows:

> The source rule for this (*ṣarf*) is the tradition of Ibn 'Umar (God be pleased with him) when he asked the Messenger of Allāh (peace be on him) saying, "I sell camels at Baqī'. Sometimes I sell them for *dīnārs* and take *dirhams* in their place and vice versa." The Messenger of Allāh (peace be on him) said, "There is no harm in this, if no further transaction is pending between you two when you separate (terminating the session)."

It is from this tradition that al-Sarakhsī derives a number of rules, especially the rule of completing the transaction of currency exchange within the session of the contract. We mention a few of the rules in the next section.

6.3 The rules of the contract of *ṣarf* are based entirely on the tradition of 'Ubādah ibn al-Ṣāmit.

We will state the most important rules here, and we will rely on al-Kāsānī for this purpose. The most significant rules are as follows:

1. *Rule 1:* Taking possession of the two counter-values exchanged prior to parting from the session of the contract. This is due to the words "from hand to hand."[33]
2. *Rule 2:* The sale of one genus with the same genus (gold for gold) or for a different genus (gold for silver) do not differ with respect to the rule of taking possession.[34]
3. *Rule 3:* If gold is exchanged for gold or silver with silver, equal for equal, and later after parting one of the parties increases the amount for the other (charges a premium), or reduces it (offers a discount) it is not permitted.[35]
4. *Rule 4:* Equality is to be maintained even if currency is exchanged for metal or metal dust.
5. *Rule 5:* The stipulation of option (*khiyār*) is not permitted in the contract of *ṣarf*.
6. *Rule 6:* There must be no delay in one counter-value or both counter-values (this the same as the rule of possession within the session of the contract).

These rules make it obvious that the tradition of 'Ubādah ibn al-Ṣāmit (R) has been applied with precision to this contract, and the contract applies to all financial transactions whether loans or currency exchange or debts.

33. Ibid., 453.
34. Ibid., 454.
35. Ibid. Imām Muḥammad in one opinion has said to have considered the discount as a future gift.

6.4 The loan transaction lies at the heart of the contract of *ṣarf*

The writings of modern scholars and express statements to the effect reveal that many of them believe that the earlier jurists did not discuss the loan transaction with interest, which is the basis of modern finance and of the banking business. It is for this reason that the lawyer representing the Government of Pakistan in the review petition of *ribā* before the Shariat Applellate Bench stated that there is no discussion of loans in Islamic law or *fiqh*. This statement can, probably, be traced back to Rashīd Riḍā. It is this belief that has led to a strange interpretation of the texts of the Qur'ān and the *Sunnah*. Such an understanding reveals that many scholars do not pay attention to the texts of the jurists or the *fiqh* manuals. It is also strange that some scholars believe that *ijtihād* is reasoning that lies outside the texts, and for this reason they call it "independent reasoning." Under this impression, they turn to commentaries on the Qur'ān and neglect the writings of the jurists. We have stated time and again that the earlier jurists are the highest authority on the interepretation of the legal texts of the Qur'ān and the *Sunnah*, and it is their texts that should be consulted first for their manuals are the primary documents on Islamic law.

The clearest example of the neglect of the writings of the jurists is the case of *ribā*. To elaborate this, we turn to one of the earliest sources on Islamic law and then to its commentary by a later jurists.

The books of Imām Muhammad al-Shaybānī (God bless him) are the first organised books on Islamic law. These books are called the *Ẓāhir al-Riwāyah* or the authentic narration of the Ḥanafī school. The content of these books was summarised by Ḥākim al-Shahīd (God bless him) in a compact book called *al-Kāfī*. The best known commentary on *al-Kāfī* is the famous book of Imām al-Sarakhsī (God bless him) called *al-Mabsūṭ*. The *matn* or the main text of this book, therefore, comes down directly from Imām Muḥammad.

This 30 volume book includes a book called *Kitāb al-Ṣarf*. Out of the 105 or so pages of this book, about 20 have been devoted to *qarḍ* (loan), and most of the concepts surrounding loans have been dealt with. Even loans in copper coins (*fulūs*) have been analysed. Later writers took out the topic of *qarḍ* and dealt with it separately. Nevertheless, Imām al-Sarakhsī's book reveals that the loans are central to the discussion of *ṣarf*, which is a contract that deals with exchange of currencies. We may reproduce some of the statements from this book to illustrate the nature of the discussion.

Structure of the Book of Sarf

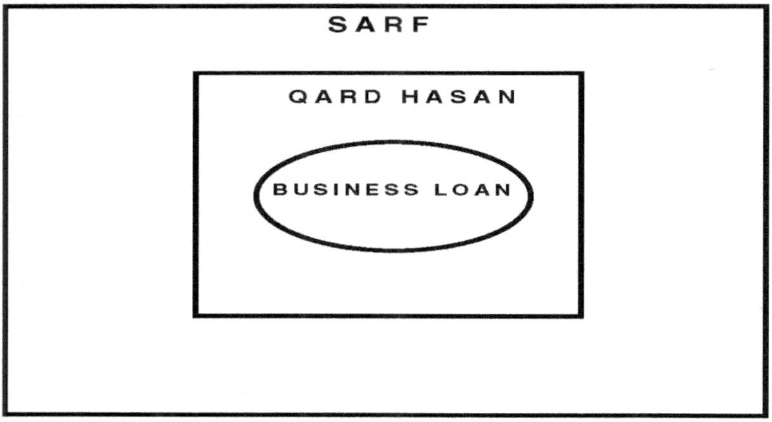

Al-Sarakhsī begins the discussion of *qarḍ* with its *ḥukm*.

> The giving of loans (*iqrāḍ*) is permitted and is recommended (*mandūb*) due to the words of the Prophet (peace be on him), "*Qarḍ* given twice is like *ṣadaqah* (of the same amount) once." The Prophet (peace be on him) said, "*Ṣadaqah* will be rewarded by ten times its amount, while *qarḍ* will have a reward of eighteen times its amount." It is said that this means that it is only the needy who seeks a loan, while *ṣadaqah* is also given to one who is not in need.

It is obvious from this statement that he is talking about what we call *qarḍ ḥasan*. A large number of cases centre around the discussion of this type of loan, that is, an interest free loan that is given by way of *iḥsān*. In this type of loan, the use of the money during the period of delay is gifted to the borrower voluntarily.

A few pages down, he makes a statement: "**The stipulation of a period is not permitted in *qarḍ*.**" This is the rule according to Ḥanafī law. After that he mentions a view attributed to Imām Mālik (God bless him) that a period can be fixed in this type of loan, because it is a debt (dayn). Al-Sarakhsī argues that it is not that type of *dayn*, for two reasons:

1. That this is a voluntary act of charity. Stipulating a period means making it binding for the person making a donation (of the period of use). Doing so will convert it into some kind of business deal and thus change it to *ribā*.

2. That *qarḍ* is like a commodate loan (*'āriyyah*) in which the amount is demanded back at will and is to be returned even if a period is fixed.

We may add to this that in *qarḍ ḥasan* the recommendation is to delay the demand for return till the borrower is enjoying financial ease. If we fix a period, this recommendation is negated and so is the purpose of the recommended act.

About the commercial loan, the following statement is explicit:

> If a person sells *dirhams* for *dirhams* with a delay and possession is given (to the borrower), the transaction stands vitiated (is *fāsid*). Due to the existence of the (two attributes of the) same genus (of the currency) and *qadr* (common method of estimation). Delay is prohibited in the case of the existence of even one of these attributes, therefore, it is more so when both attributes are found.

There are other statements too. It is to be noted that he mentions the word "sale" here and not *qarḍ*, although he is talking about *qarḍ*, within the topic of *qarḍ*, because the term *qarḍ* implies *iḥsān* and donation, while the term sale implies a business deal. To use the term *qarḍ* in this statement he would have had to say: " If a person gives a loan of *dirhams*, as a business deal, to be returned in *dirhams*, and possession is given (to the borrower), the transaction stands vitiated (is *fāsid*)."

We need not dwell further on the issue, as it is clear, but we do need to explain the term debt (*dayn*) in a little more detail as that causes confusion in the minds of readers.

6.5 The loan transaction creates one type of dayn, but there are other transactions through which debt is created.

We have stated above that Imām Mālik (God bless him) considers the giving of *qarḍ* as a debt (*dayn*), while Imām al-Sarakhsī argues that it is not a debt arising out of a business deal; it is a different type of debt. We, therefore, need to see how many types of debts can arise through business transactions and how is *qarḍ* different from them.

The figure below tries to present a simplified meaning of debts. Others may go into details and identify further classifications. Let us give brief explanations for each type:

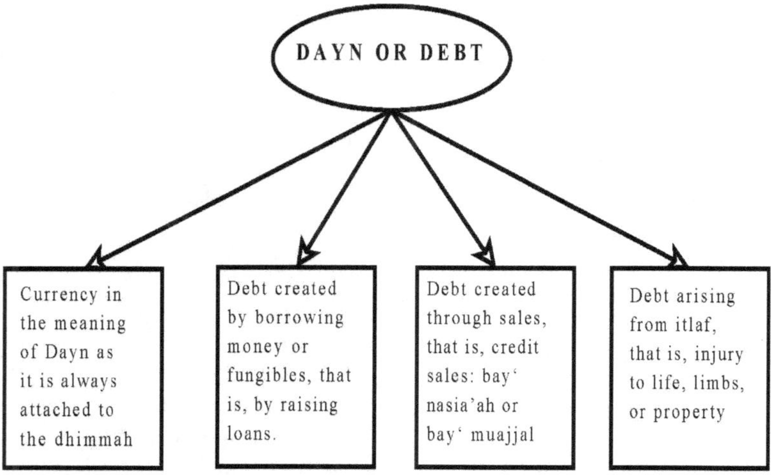

1. **Absolute currencies in the meaning of *dayn* (debt).** In the chart on the types of *bay'* that we produced above, the types of *bay'* are stated as *dayn* with *'ayn*, *dayn* with *dayn* and so forth. Here *dayn* means absolute currencies or *dīnārs* and *dirhams*. Currencies are called *dayn*, because at the time of making a contract they are attached to the *dhimmah* as a liability by merely mentioning their number. The currency does not have to be shown to the other party or ascertained. Ascertainment means checking the weight or measure of the counter-value offered. As currencies are pre-standardized, they do no have to be weighed each time a contract is made. If a party is buying something for ten *dīnārs*, delivery is made to him and he becomes liable for paying ten *dīnārs*. The *dīnārs* do not have to be present at the time of the contract. Anything that is present is called *'ayn*, while the counter-value not present and is pre-ascertained is called *dayn*.

2. **Loans borrowed for business create debts, but these are prohibited.** These are of three types:

    a) *Qarḍ Hasan*. This is permitted, but it is a charitable loan. It is about this transaction that the Qur'ān says: "If the borrower is in a difficulty, grant him time till it is easy for him to repay. But if ye remit it by way of charity, that is best for you if ye only knew."[36]

36. Qur'ān 2:280

b) *Loan without interest.* This is a business loan and is not referred to as *qarḍ* by the jurists, but a sale of a currency in return for a currency of the same denomination or of a different denomination where the value is equal. This is not permitted due to *ribā al-nasī'ah.*

c) *Loan with interest.* This is a business loan and is not referred to as *qarḍ* by the jurists, but a sale of a currency in return for a currency of the same denomination or of a different denomination where the value is in excess and includes interest. This is not permitted due to *ribā al-nasī'ah* as well as *ribā al-faḍl.*

3. **Debts created through credit sales.** A credit sale is one in which the payment (usually currency) for the thing bought is delayed. It is called *bay' al-nasī'ah* by the jurists, but these days the term *bay' mu'ajjal* or deferred sale is preferred. The credit sale is permitted in Islamic law, but with certain conditions. "O ye who believe! When ye deal in debts (*dayn*) for specified periods of delay, reduce them to writing."[37] The words "specified period" distinguish it from the meaning of *dayn* in the meaning of currency mentioned at number one. This meaning is clarified by the words, "But if it is spot trade taking place among you, there is no sin for you if do not reduce it to writing."[38] Here the *dayn* (currency) is not for a specified period. The credit sale is the real creator of *dayn* in business transactions. It was this debt that was "doubled and multiplied" due to non-payment. According to al-Sarakhsī, in the words of Ibn 'Abbās (God be pleased with him) the verse applies to the *salam* contract. That too will create a debt.

4. **Debts may be created through destruction of property or life and limbs.** Payments become due through *itlāf,* and due to *diyāt* and other reasons.

---

37. Qur'ān 2:282. The reader should not that the English term "debt" always implies a delayed period, so what does a "debt for a specified period" mean here.
38. Qur'ān 2:282

6.6 Only one type of loan transaction is permitted and that is the transaction called *qarḍ ḥasan*, which is actually a charitable act and not a business transaction. This creates a problem for Islamic banking as it is practised today.

From all that has preceded, we can conclude that cash loans are not allowed in Islamic law. The only loan allowed is the *qarḍ ḥasan*. In fact, business loans are not even referred to as *qarḍ*, but sale of currency. For this reason, Imām al-Sarakhsī points out that "The *qarḍ*, even though it is in the meaning of *bay'*, because it is the passing of ownership in property, it is not sale in reality." In other words, the business loans are sale, but the *qarḍ ḥasan* differs.

Conventional banking, however, is based on the concept of a loan. From the opening of a bank account right up to the financing of huge projects. If the loan transaction is not permitted, conventional banking will have to shut down. Islamic banks and the scholars justifying the products used by Islamic banks are, therefore, eager to preserve the permissibility of the business loan. To do so they equate it with *qarḍ ḥasan*, but it is not possible to do so.

A persual of the standards laid down by the AOIFI shows that the loan transaction is utilised wherever possible. Let us quote from the standard on currencies.

> 2/3 It is also prohibited to deal in the forward currency market even if the purpose is hedging to avoid a loss of profit on a particular transaction effected in a currency whose value is expected to decline.
>
> 2/4 It is permissible for the institution to hedge against the future devaluation of the currency by recourse to the following:
>
> (a) **To execute back to back interest free loans using different currencies without receiving or giving an extra benefit, provided these two loans are not contractually conncected to each other.**
>
> (b) Where the exposure is in respect of an account payable, to sell goods on credit or by Murabaha in the currency of the exposure.

We are sorry to disappoint them, but the transaction highlighted above is not lawful according to the rules elaborated in detail in this book.

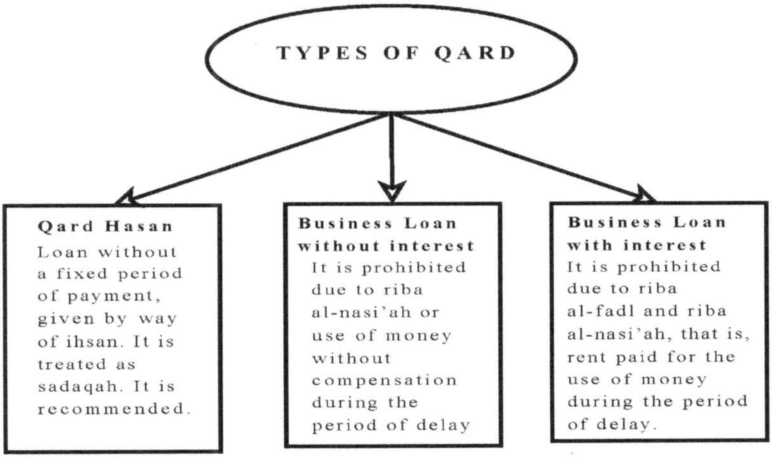
TYPES OF QARD
Qard Hasan
Loan without a fixed period of payment, given by way of ihsan. It is treated as sadaqah. It is recommended.
Business Loan without interest
It is prohibited due to riba al-nasi'ah or use of money without compensation during the period of delay
Business Loan with interest
It is prohibited due to riba al-fadl and riba al-nasi'ah, that is, rent paid for the use of money during the period of delay.

Let us quote from al-Sarakhsī to show that a *muḍārib* cannot raise a business loan.

> (Suppose) he orders him to raise debts through *istidānah* against the wealth (of the *muḍārabah*) or against the credit of the *rabb al-māl,* and he does so purchasing a slave girl for the *muḍārabah.* Thereafter, he raises a loan (*qarḍ*) of a thousand *dirhams* against the *muḍārabah* and purchases a(nother) slave girl with it. This second purchase is deemed to be for his personal account, and he is personally liable for the *qarḍ.* Among the jurists are those who say that *istidānah* pertains to purchase on credit, and raising of loans (*qarḍ*) is something different. It (raising of cash loans), therefore, is not included in an unqualified authority of *istidānah.* **The correct view is to say that granting the authority to raise loans is *bāṭil* (void).**
>
> Do you not see that if he had ordered a person to raise a loan of one thousand for him from a certain person, and the person did so the one thousand would be for the person raising the loan and not for the one who ordered him. The reason is that *qarḍ* is compensated with a similar (*mithl*) fungible and is a liability of the borrower. If the counter-value is his liability, the borrower becomes the owner of the *qarḍ,* and he is in no need of the command of another for doing this. Giving

> an order for raising a loan is identical to giving an order for begging, which is *bāṭil*. Whatever is obtained through begging belongs to the beggar and not to another. Once this is established, we may say that whatever the *muḍārib* raises as a loan goes into his personal ownership."[39]

Commenting on the above passage from al-Sarakhsī, we made the following statement (two paras) in our book on *Partnerships:*

This passage explains to us that there is no concept of a business loan in Islamic law. All that is acknowledged is a charitable loan, which is identical to begging. Even when a charitable loan is raised it does not belong to the business; it is owned personally by the borrower, and he alone is liable for it personally. Even if we were to acknowledge that a business firm, as a juristic person, may raise an interest free loan for itself, the problem would be that no period of repayment can be fixed for it, and the corporation may be asked to pay it back the next day.[40] Business cannot function this way.

This concept of Islamic law has devastating consequences for many of the schemes of banking and finance designed by modern institutions on the recommendations of modern scholars. Islamic business has to be a loan free business; it has to be based on the principles of true participation.

This comment was made in 1996, but we consider it to be valid even today. The footnote has been added now.

6.7 The *Sharī'ah* Standards of the AIOFI by not following the rules of *ṣarf* with precision suffer from some glaring contradictions.

The Shari'ah Standards have been made by AIOFI and there is an impressive list of scholars on their board. The scholars mentioned in the list have made or approved these standards. The Standards are a result of hard work and we do appreciate the prolonged deliberations this must have required. Nevertheless, some of the standards suffer from defects. In particular, some statements have been made that have not

39. Al-Sarakhsī, *al-Mabsūṭ*, vol. 22, p. 180.
40. We may add here that the corporation cannot utilise this loan for the benefit of the shareholders.

been checked for analytical consistency. Here we will just indicate two, because they are relevant to the business loan that we have stated is not permitted under Islamic law.

6.7.1 Standard on trading in currencies and the business loan

The Shari'ah Standard on trading in currencies makes the following statement:

> 2/1 It is permissible to trade in currencies provided that it is done in compliance with the following Shari'a rules and precepts:
>
> (a) Both parties must take possession of the countervalues before dispersing, such possession being either actual or constructive.
>
> (b) **The counter values of the same currency must be of equal amount even if one of them is in paper money and the other is in coin of the same country, like a note of one pound for a coin of one pound.**
>
> (c) The contract shall not contain any conditional option or deferment clause regarding the delivery of one or both counter values.
>
> (d) The dealing in currencies shall not aim at establishing a monopoly position, nor should it entail any evil consequences to the interest of individuals or societies.
>
> (e) Currency transactions shall not be carried out on the forward or futures market.

Examine the statement highlighted above carefully. It says: "**The counter values of the same currency must be of equal amount even if one of them is in paper money and the other is in coin of the same country, like a note of one pound for a coin of one pound.**" Examine it in the light of the rule that precedes it and requires immediate exchange of the counter-values. We raise the question: If the counter-values of the same currency are (1) to be exchanged at once and (2) to be made equal, then how do you justify a loan? If you follow this rule, you cannot even justify the *qarḍ ḥasan*.

The truth is that the statements within the contract of *ṣarf*, its conditions, have just been reproduced without analysis and reflection; without relating the principles and rules of Islamic law.

What we are saying is that the statement above, made by AIOFI, prohibits loans, whether they are based on interest or they are without interest. Yet, they go ahead as if these loans are permitted.

6.7.2 Standard on trading on *salam* and the business loan

It is well known that the *salam* contract is not permitted in currencies. *Salam* is advance payment and this would amount to paying a currency for a currency. Thus, an advance payment of $100 is not allowed for $100 (or 110 and so on) to be delivered after a period. *Salam* is not permitted even if wheat, for example, is being delivered as advance payment (see above under *salam* as an exception).

The Shari'ah Standard number 10 on *salam*, acknowledges the first part of this rule, and states at item 3/24:

> It is not permissible for a *muslam fihi* to be an amount of currency or gold or silver, if the capital of the *salam* contract was paid in the form of currency or gold or silver.

The *muslam fihi* is the currency, gold, or silver, as the case may be, to be delivered after a period.

The obvious question we raise here is: **If one currency cannot be paid for another currency, gold for gold, or silver for silver, then how is the loan transaction justified; whether the loan is with or without interest?**

6.7.3 The usual responses we get

When we raise these and other questions, the first response we get is that the translation into English does not appear to be correct. The reality is that this response is incorrect, as the Arabic text conveys the same meaning.

The second response we get is: these rules are independent, and the rules for loans are independent. This response may be acceptable from someone who understands neither *fiqh* nor law—a total layman—but not from a scholar. We are sure that even laymen, using their common sense, will say that the rules should be analytical consistent and must be woven into intitial rules and exceptions (*azīmah* and *rukhṣah*).

CHAPTER 7

DEFINING *RIBĀ* AND DETERMINING THE RULES FOR *RIBĀ* IN TRANSACTIONS

Some years ago, we defined *ribā* in the light of the texts discussed above. The rules derived in the previous chapters were incorporated into the definition, and the definition was drafted in the form of a section of a code. The definition is reproduced here. The definition is preceded by four rules that were also derived from the rules emerging from the texts and the other rules of *fiqh*. These rules help identify transactions in which *ribā* exists. The definition is followed by illustrations to which the rules are applied. Taken together, the rules, the definition and the illustrations should serve as a short primer on the meaning of *ribā*.

The text written a few years ago began with the following assumptions:

Since the institutions in Muslim countries are reluctant, for whatever reason, to provide a definition of *ribā*, it becomes the duty of individuals to do so. In the following few pages, we propose to do three things:

1. to list a few simple rules of *ribā* derived by Muslim jurists for identifying *ribā*-bearing transactions;
2. to propose a definition that conforms with the views of the earlier jurists;
3. to give some illustrations that should enable any reader to understand, with a little mental effort, not only the definition provided, but also the proper meaning of *ribā* as expounded by the earlier jurists.

These were the three tasks, and they are the subject-matter of this chapter.

7.1 If four conditions are met in a transaction, it is to be declared a *ribā*-bearing transaction. These conditions are also called the four rules of *ribā*.

An examination of the work of the earlier jurists, discussed in the previous chapters, reveals four basic rules or conditions for *ribā*. We can call them conditions, because *all four must be met in a transaction before such a transaction can be called usurious*. The rules are first stated below and then each rule is explained briefly.

1. A usurious transaction involves the exchange of two counter-values.
2. *Ribā* is found when ownership in the item exchanged is passed on to the other party.
3. *Ribā* is found when the items exchanged are the same or are species of the same genus.
4. An excess (based on weight and measure, or on period of delay) must be found and passed on to the other party either in one of the exchanged items or in both.

7.1.1 Rule 1: A usurious transaction involves the exchange of two counter-values.

This rule reflects the meaning of the term *bay'*, that is, exchange of two counter-values. A loan too is included in this meaning, because a loan there is an exchange of two counter-values and these are currency-values. If A gives 100 dollars to B, which B promptly returns after a few days, the transaction would be affected by this rule as it is an exchange of two counter-values. A gift, on the other hand, is not covered by this rule nor is a bequest, because there is no counter-value (compensation) in these transactions.

7.1.2 Rule 2: *Ribā* is found when ownership in the item exchanged is passed on to the other party.

This rule is stated on many occasions in the books of *fiqh*, but one place where it appears most clearly is where a distinction is drawn between a commodate loan, which is a loan of utensils and other household things borrowed, and *qarḍ*, which is a loan of a fungible without interest and without a fixed period of repayment. If A gives his horse to B for use, and B returns the horse after a few days, the exchange is not affected by this rule (nor by the previous rule), because the ownership in the horse was not passed on to B. If A deposits 100 dīnārs with B and B locks them up in a safe, returning the same dīnārs to A on demand, the rule does not apply, because ownership in the dīnārs belongs to A.

If, however, A gives 100 dīnārs to B for his use and B uses them in his business or for his needs and then returns 100 dīnārs to A, the transaction is hit by the rule, because ownership in the dīnārs passed to B as soon as he used them. This is visualized in the loan of a fungible commodity. If A takes a loan of 100 kilograms of wheat from B, the ownership in the wheat passes on to A as soon as he consumes the wheat or sells it. He is now liable to B for 100 kilograms of wheat of a similar quantity; he cannot return the original wheat as that stands consumed or is no longer in his possession. The same thing happens in a *qarḍ* of money. On the other hand, if A borrows B's car he is bound to return the same car and not another one of the same quality or make.

This rule rule highlights the passing of ownership in *mithlīs* or fungibles, which are things that are similar or can be returned through substitutes. Thus, 100 standardized dīnārs are the same as any other 100 standardized dīnārs or 100 kilos of wheat are the same as another 100 kilos of wheat of the same quality. These commodities are to be paid back in their substitutes and the substance itself is not to be returned; in fact, it cannot be because it has been consumed by use.

The rule also highlights the difference between rent and interest. When I rent my house, in which I invested a 100,000 dollars, to a tenant, ownership in the house does not pass to the tenant; he only gets the right to use the house. If, on the other hand, I rent out a 100,000 dollars as an investment to someone and ask him to pay rent on these dollars, it amounts to interest or *ribā* as ownership in the dollars passed on to the other person as soon as he used them.

7.1.3 Rule 3: *Ribā* is found when the items exchanged are the same or are species of the same genus.

The first part is easy to understand, that is, when the items are the same. Thus, *ribā* may be found in a transaction where gold is exchanged for gold (the same precious metal), or when silver is exchanged for silver, or when dollars are exchanged for dollars.

As for the second part about the genus and specie, it would be useful to look briefly at the contract of *ṣarf*. It is a contract that governs all transactions in currencies, loan transactions and precious metals, and is based on the genus determined through weight or currency-value.

The law designed by the *fuqahā'*, and discussed in the previous chapters, to deal with *ribā* in currencies and loans is called the contract of *ṣarf* and is based upon the texts of the Qur'ān and the *Sunnah.* This contract covers all transactions in currencies and in precious metals like gold and silver. Thus, it applies to the activity of the *ṣarrāf:* a banker, a money-changer and a jeweller. *The simple requirement of the contract is that all transactions in currencies or in precious metals be spot, that is, the two currencies (or currency-values) in the transaction must be exchanged immediately and without delay.* Another requirement of the contract is that if the exchange is in the same currency (for example dīnārs for dīnārs or dollars for dollars), no excess can be paid from either side. The contract covers, as already stated, all banking transactions including deposits, withdrawals and loans. This appears to be an obvious reason why the banking business, as it exists today, was not developed by Muslim merchants and businessmen.

Thus, if A gives 1000 dollars to B on the condition that he pay back 1100 dollars after one year, the contract of *ṣarf* would say:

1. Make them equal, that is, exchange 1000 dollars for 1000 dollars and not for 1100. This prohibits what we usually call interest.
2. After obeying the first instruction, we are left with what may be called an interest free loan: exchange of 1000 dollars with 1000 dollars with a delay of one year. The contract of *ṣarf* does not permit this; it requires the transaction to be spot. The dollars will have to be exchanged at once, which appears futile, however, the goal of the prohibition stands achieved. The reason why it does not permit this is explained in the next rule.

These conditions were elaborated in the discussion of the tradition of 'Ubādah ibn al-Ṣāmit above.

7.1.4 Rule 4: An excess must be found and passed on to the other party either in one of the exchanged items or in both.

Ribā is expressed in terms of excess. This excess is of two types. The first type of excess is estimated through weight or measure. Thus, if 100 grams of gold are exchanged for 110 grams of gold, the excess is 10 grams. The second type of excess is estimated on the basis of delay in the delivery of an item. We may recall al-Sarakhsī's statement here:

"The Prophet's words, 'And the excess (*faḍl*) is *ribā*,' imply *faḍl* (excess) through *qadr* (estimation) and they imply *faḍl* (excess) through a period of delay, with one being paid in cash and the other by way of *nasī'ah*, and each one of them is intended.' " The words "without a counter-value," therefore, imply either the absence of a counter-value or the existence of a counter-value that is not legal. It is the potential benefit that can be derived through the delayed item during the period of delay. This is what is called the time value of money in modern finance. As indicated earlier, in Islamic law, the first type of excess is called *ribā al-faḍl* and the second type is called *ribā al-nasī'ah*. *Ribā al-nasī'ah is, therefore, the time value of money.*

These, then, are the four rules of *ribā* that can be gleaned from any book of the earlier jurists, especially the Ḥanafīs. Let us now convert these rules into a workable definition.

7.2 The texts on *ribā* and the writings of the jurists yield a comprehensive definition of *ribā*.

The definition proposed here represents a strict traditional position in conformity with the teachings of Islamic law, but it is not comprehensive insofar as it covers transactions in currencies and precious metals (gold and silver) alone. The definition, therefore, is based upon the contract of *ṣarf* and does not apply to everything that falls under the purview of the prohibition of *ribā* in *fiqh* literature. In case, a comprehensive definition is desired, one that applies to everything measured and weighed as explained in the rules above, the word "counter-value" should be substituted for the word "currency-value" in the text of the definition that follows.

The definition assumes that paper money is not to be treated as an acknowledgment of a debt (which it actually is), but as commodity money, that is, currency minted from gold and silver. Questions of inflation and indexation are, therefore, eliminated.[41] For the sake of precision, the definition has been framed in the form of provisions of a code of law.

The definition is stated in four sections and their accompanying explanations.

§1. *Ribā* is of two types: manifest and concealed.

41. This means that the solutions to the problems of inflation, aggravated due to the prohibition *ribā*, lie elsewhere and not in indexation.

§2. Manifest *Ribā* is

(1) *ribā al-faḍl*, which is the excess stipulated in the exchange of two currency-values of the same specie, whether the transaction is spot or delayed, and/or

(2) *ribā al-nasī'ah*, which is the potential benefit to be derived during the period of delay stipulated for either of the exchanged currency-values.

Explanation 1: The word "excess" means an excess revealed through weighing for gold and silver and by count for paper currency. The word "exchange" means transfer of ownership in the currency-value exchanged. A "spot" transaction is one in which both currency-values are exchanged in a single session (*majlis*). The word "delayed" applies to the period of delay stipulated for the delivery of one of the exchanged currency-values, however, the delivery of both currency-values may be delayed in which case the word includes a futures transaction.

Explanation 2: Fiat money (paper money), gold and silver belong to three different species, but to the same genus called currency-value. Currencies of two countries belong to two different species, but have the same genus called currency-value. Wrought gold and gold dust are a single specie as are wrought silver and silver dust, but gold and silver, whatever their form, belong to the same genus called currency-value.

Explanation 3: The rules of *ribā al-faḍl* apply within the same specie, while those of *ribā al-nasī'ah* apply within the same genus as well.

Explanation 4: *Qarḍ ḥasan* is an exchange of two currency-values with a delay in which the period of delay is not fixed and the potential benefit derived during the delayed period (time value) is consciously gifted to the beneficiary. It is, therefore, an exception to §2(2) obtained by keeping the period of repayment open.

§3. *Ribā* is concealed when the primary objective of two or more related transactions is the same as that of a single transaction of manifest *ribā*.

§4. *Ribā*, whether manifest or concealed, is prohibited and all transactions involving *ribā* are void.

Explanation: According to the Ḥanafī school, transactions involving *ribā* are not void, but vitiated, and they can become valid if the offending condition is removed.

7.3 The four rules of *ribā* and the definition can be applied very easily to illustrations that identify the transactions of *ribā*

The definition is now followed by illustrations that highlight certain important, yet simple, transactions. Each transaction mentioned in the illustrations is linked to a provision in the definition, which in turn can be traced to a *ḥadīth*. Some of the prohibitions emerging through the illustrations may be quite shocking for some, but the reader should try to visualize the whole system rather than a few details here and there.

The illustrations are based upon simple transactions. A complex transaction, especially one in foreign currency, should be analyzed into its simple components and subjected to the same rules.

7.3.1 Time deposit with interest

A, an individual, deposits $ 10,000 with B, a banker, on the understanding that A will not demand the money from B before a period of one year and in lieu of which A will receive 12% interest. The transaction, in different words, is an exchange of currency for currency with an excess and a stipulated delay. The transaction is void, because it contains an excess of 12% in one currency-value over the other currency-value of the same specie (the excess is called *ribā al-faḍl*). It is also void because it contains a potential benefit to be derived from the use of the money for one year (the excess in the form of a potential benefit, the time value of money, is called *ribā al-nasī'ah*). This is the normal transaction of *ribā*, and in such a transaction the benefit of 12% interest goes to A, while the potential benefit to be derived from the use of the money during the period of delay goes to B. Some economists would call interest charged in this transaction as rent for money. In such a case, *ribā al-faḍl* is the rent for *ribā al-nasī'ah*. A transaction for acquiring money on rent is exactly what is prohibited.

7.3.2 Bank deposit and withdrawal

A, an individual, deposits $ 10,000 with B, a bank on the first day of the month. A withdraws $ 10,000 on the last day of the month (or on any other day). The transaction is an exchange of currency for currency of the same specie with a delay and, therefore, amounts to *ribā* (under section 2(2) above) irrespective of whether any interest was paid to A by

B. The basis of prohibition is that there is a potential benefit to be derived by B from $ 10,000 during the month (this is called *ribā al-nasī'ah*). There are two ways in which this transaction will be permitted: (1) If A deposits the money on the understanding that he is giving a *qarḍ ḥasan* to B, the bank. The rules of *qarḍ ḥasan* will apply.[42] (2) If A deposits the money on the understanding that it is a *wadī'ah* (deposit). In such a case, B cannot use the currency notes and will have to return the same currency notes to A on demand. This would amount to keeping the currency notes in a locker for A. In other words, the currency-values have not been exchanged in the sense of transfer of ownership, and A always retains ownership in the money deposited. If A gives permission to B to use the currency notes in the banking business, the contract of *wadī'ah* will be converted to one of agency and B will become an agent acting on behalf of A, thus, A will be liable for any loss resulting from B's handling of the funds.[43] If profits are to be shared by the principal and agent, the contract will become one of *muḍārabah.*

7.3.3 Interest-free loan

Z gives a loan of $ 10,000 to A and asks him to repay the loan after one year. Z does not demand any interest. The transaction is void as it contains a potential benefit to be derived during a period of delay that is stipulated. The benefit will go to A without any compensation for Z. This is unjustified enrichment. If Z does not stipulate any period of repayment, the transaction is valid as *qarḍ ḥasan,* which amounts to a conscious gifting of the benefits to A within the meaning of Explanation 4 to §2. In such a case, it is recommended that Z demand repayment when A is enjoying financial ease, however, Z is at liberty to demand repayment whenever she likes.

7.3.4 Interest-free loan with a service charge

B, a banker, gives an interest-free loan to E, an entrepreneur, for a period of three years. B stipulates the condition that E will pay each year a service charge amounting to 20% of the amount advanced. The transaction is void, because a period of repayment has been stipulated. It is also

42. Imagine a poor worker giving a charitable loan to a bank.
43. According to some jurists, if B uses the funds without such permission from A, the rules of usurpation will apply to B's act and he will be liable to compensate A, that is, return the money, but keep the profits earned.

void, because *ribā* in the form of 20% excess has been stipulated. This excess amounts to a benefit arising from an interest-free loan. To make the transaction valid, the conditions pertaining to the fixed period of repayment and the service charge should be dropped. This will convert it into a *qarḍ ḥasan*.

7.3.5 Bank advance on the basis of *murābaḥah*

E, an employee, requests his banker B receiving his monthly salary, to advance him a loan amounting to three salaries. B agrees and advances a loan of $ 20,000 to E recoverable in 12 monthly installments of $ 2000 each. The repayment includes a mark-up of $ 4000 recoverable in one year. The transaction is void, because it is an exchange of currency for currency not only with a stipulated period of repayment, but also with a stipulated excess. The transaction is void even if the demand for the mark-up is given up. The only way this transaction is valid is when B drops the condition of mark-up and does not stipulate a period of repayment, that is, keeps it open. This will convert it into a *qarḍ ḥasan*.

7.3.6 The buy-back agreement

B sells an item to Z for $ 10,000 paid in cash. After the cash is paid, Z sells the same item back to B for $ 12,000 to be paid after one year. The two transactions are void, because their combined purpose is to conceal a transaction of *ribā*. Whether this was really the intention of B and Z is a question of fact, however, if Z is a banker, the presumption would be that she is giving a loan to B on interest.

7.3.7 Buying gold or gold ornaments with currency

A, a customer, pays $ 10,000 to J, a jeweller, for the delivery of a gold ring (or for gold coins). J promises to deliver the ring after two weeks. The transaction is void due to delay in delivery of the gold ring. The reason is that a potential benefit is being derived from a currency-value (that is of a different specie, but of the same genus) for a period of two weeks, The exchange must take place within the same session of the contract, which depends upon commercial practice. Whether A can pay an advance to J against craftsmanship is a separate issue.[44]

44. The OIC has issued a ruling on this issue that is quite vague.

7.3.8 Exchange of currencies

Z pays to F, a foreign currency dealer, an amount of US $1000 on the condition that Z will change it for Rs. 37500. F takes the dollars and asks Z to come back the next day for her money payable in rupees. The transaction is void. The exchange of the two currencies should take place in the same session of the contract. As to what is a session for such a contract is a question of fact depending upon commercial practice.

7.3.9 Investing in a partnership

A, an entrepreneur, gives $ 10,000 to B, another entrepreneur, on the understanding that B will use the money and share the profits with A. After a period of one year B returns $ 12,000 to A informing him that the amount includes his principal and share of profits. Apparently this transaction should be void, because two currency-values have been exchanged and an excess has been returned with the other counter-value after a delay of one year. The transaction, however, is not void on the ground that A always retained ownership in the $ 10,000 paid and B was using it on his behalf as an agent or partner.[45]

7.3.10 Investing in the ordinary shares of a corporation

A, an individual, subscribes to the capital of C, a company registered under the Pakistani Companies Ordinance, 1984 having the liability of its members limited to the extent of their shares (called a corporation in the United States). A buys 100 shares having a face-value of Rs. 10 each. After one year, C pays a dividend of twelve percent and agrees to redeem the shares owned by A at face-value (assuming for a moment that this is possible, because in practice it is not). The transaction is void, because this is an exchange of two currency-values with an excess after a period of delay. In this transaction, unlike a partnership, the ownership of the subscribed capital of $ 10,000 passed on to C, a juristic person in whose assets A did not become a co-owner. The problem can be overcome through *ijtihād*, but the same cannot be said about debentures and bonds.

45. The American Uniform Partnership Act now favors the entity concept even for the partnership. This will have the same ruling as in the next illustration.

7.3.11 Pension fund or provident fund

E, an employee, authorizes his employer, M, to deduct a fixed amount each month from his salary as a contribution toward a provident fund for employees. M agrees to refund the contributed amount alongwith profits earned by the fund at the end of E's service. M also agrees to make a similar contribution toward E's fund and to pay the amount contributed alongwith profits earned at the end of E's service. The transaction is valid if E retains ownership of his own contribution and is also liable for the entire loss that may result from M's handling of the funds. The reason for the validity of this transaction is that an exchange of currency-values has not taken place and E retains ownership of his own contribution. M is handling the funds as an agent. The contribution by M to the fund is a separate transaction and amounts to a gift to E at the end of his service.

CHAPTER 8

COUNTING THE *FULŪS* (COPPER COINS) AND FIAT CURRENCY

A major issue that needs *ijtihād* is that of fiat currency or paper money issued by governments. We have discussed this issue earlier in our book called *The Concept of Ribā*. Tariq al-Dewany has done some excellent work on the issue of currency and that should be examined. Nevertheless, if paper currency is to be considered currency proper then it must be subjected to the rules that apply to *dīnārs* and *dirhams*. The AIOFI in its standard on trading in currencies has already assumed, without discussion, that paper currency is like *dīnārs* and *dirhams*, and is to be subjected to the same rules. We reproduce the quotation produced above to illustrate this point.

> 2/1 It is permissible to trade in currencies provided that it is done in compliance with the following Shari'a rules and precepts:
>
> (a) Both parties must take possession of the countervalues before dispersing, such possession being either actual or constructive.
>
> (b) **The counter values of the same currency must be of equal amount even if one of them is in paper money and the other is in coin of the same country, like a note of one pound for a coin of one pound.**
>
> (c) The contract shall not contain any conditional option or deferment clause regarding the delivery of one or both counter values.
>
> (d) The dealing in currencies shall not aim at establishing a monopoly position, nor should it entail any evil consequences to the interest of individuals or societies.
>
> (e) Currency transactions shall not be carried out on the forward or futures market.

Here paper currency is being treated like the currencies of gold and silver and is being subjected to the same rules. In our book mentioned in the previous paragraph, we had made the following statement:

> To avoid the restrictions of the contract of *ṣarf,* some Muslim economists, who have not examined the rules of *fiqh,* are trying to say that the rules for currency transactions developed in *fiqh* are not applicable to modern paper currency, thus, transactions with a delay including futures transactions should be permitted in paper currency. This is an erroneous assumption. It is the unanimous opinion of jurists, both classical and modern, that anything used as currency will be subject to the rule of *ribā,* even when it is made of something such as leather.
>
> The truth is that paper currency will have to be treated as commodity money for the rules of *ribā.* The only other option is to take it for what it really is, an acknowledgement of a debt, a promissory note. This, however, will prohibit most transactions in paper currency, because the exchange of a debt for a debt is strictly and unanimously prohibited in Islamic law.

After this, some suggested that modern currency is like copper coins (*fulūs*). Copper coins were accepted as currency due to the need of the people. Paper currency, they argue has been accepted for the same reason, therefore, the rules applicable to copper coins should be applied to paper currency. The most important rule that makes this suggestion attractive is the statement of Imām Muḥammad al-Shaybānī (God bless him), who records the preferred view of the school: "There is no harm in *salam* in *fulūs* (copper coins) when they are sold by count." As pointed out above, the jurists did not allow *salam* in *dīnārs* and *dirhams,* that is, as the delayed commodity, but they are permitting it in *fulūs.*

This, however, is looking at the surface and assuming that copper coins and paper currency are similar. The legal reasoning that follows the statement has not been examined by those who hold copper coins to be similar to fiat currency. The explanation says: "Because they closely resemble countable items (like walnuts and eggs in which *salam* is allowed) or they are a fungible commodity." In other words, copper coins usually take the rule of copper metal, especially when they are demonetized or in case of dispute. They have an intrinsic value and they revert to copper metal for the purpose. Paper currency has no intrinsic value. Here we should note the opinion of Imām Muḥammad al-Shaybānī himself, because his opinion differs from the preferred opinion in the school. He says that copper coins should be treated as currency proper and *salam* should not be allowed in them. The two senior jurists disagree with this and maintain that they are a useful device, but will take the rule of metal in case of problems. Accordingly, our statement in the previous book, "It is the unanimous opinion of jurists, both classical and modern, that anything used as currency will be subject to the rule of *ribā*, even when it is made of something such as leather," still holds true. *Fulūs* are not "currency proper." This should be enough to show that the rules should be examined thoroughly before reaching conclusions.

CHAPTER 9

CONCLUSION ABOUT ISLAMIC BANKING

The rules described above strike at the heart of banking, an consequently Islamic banking as it is practised today. This is especially true of the rule that raising cash loans for business is not allowed, unless it is the *qarḍ ḥasan* that does not have a fixed period of repayment and depends upon the ability of the borrower to pay. The same rule also hits the opening of bank accounts. Modern banking laws function on the basis of the rule that all bank accounts are opened on the basis of a "loan given to the bank." What we call "deposits" are loans given to banks. According to the rules elaborated above, these loans and accounts cannot be permitted. The bank also cannot be given a *qarḍ ḥasan*, for banks are there to make money for their shareholders and are not in the charity or begging business. In addition to this, the *qarḍ ḥasan* does not accept the concept of agency (*wakālah*); each person has to beg for himself and raise a charitable loan. If the above rules are applied, as they should be, it spells huge problems for the Islamic banking business.

This is not to say that we do not appreciate the efforts being made by Muslims to promote Islamic banking. We are sure that some people sincerely believe that the way Islamic banks are functioning is the sound way, and the products they are selling are "shariah compatible." We hope that such sincere people will reconsider the rules for themselves and not listen to what others have to say.

There have been observations by people that Islamic banking as it is practised today has had little or no impact on the lives and commerce of the people. The claims of distributive justice have come to nought. In response to such observations, some scholars have stated that we are passing through a transition phase. The set of rules that are being followed are not the true rules, and these will be replaced by a new set of rules as Islamic banking progressess and flourishes. We have to disagree with this philosophy for the following reason: The rules have a chance of improving if you are aiming for your target, but miss it for some unavoidable reasons. If, however, you are aiming in a totally wrong direction then there is no chance of your hitting the desired target. We feel that the advocates of Islamic banking have their arrows pointed in the wrong direction.

There are those who fail to recognize that there is a no difference between conventional banking and the present Islamic banking. They maintain, and try to convince others, that the difference is clear when you consider the difference between an animal that is slaughtered, according to the Islamic rites, and one that is not. It would be a good explanation if only the animal slaughtered was a neutral animal, but the analogy is not useful if the animal being slaughtered ritually unhealthy or is carrion.

As stated above, current Islamic banking has had no impact on the lives of the people with respect to the fair sharing or resources or distributive justice. How can it when these banks follow the same philosophy that is followed by conventional banks. Most of the products are the same with Arabic names. It is for this reason that it is so easy for Western banks to offer "shariah compatible" products and call it Islamic banking. In fact, some of the so called "shariah compatible" products may be more expensive for the custormers.

If Islamic banking has to become Islamic the idea of "cash loans" has to go. In other words, the concept of credit has to be altered radically and the creation of fake money by the banks has to come to an end. Till this is done, it will be difficult to call these banks "Islamic." The obvious question that will be raised is: Will such banking be banking? Maybe not, and in our view this is not important as long as a system that is truly Islamic is put into place. We feel that even though the banking industry in Muslim countries is dominated and remotely controlled by Western banks, it is possible to have truly Islamic banks or institutions that perform similar services.

We also feel that a constructive step in this direction may be to revive the Islamic *dirham* and *dinār*. We believe that considerable work has been done in this direction already.

ABOUT THIS BOOK

The texts of the Qur'ān and the *Sunnah* that prohibit *ribā* are not easy to understand. An earlier book written by this author, called *The Concept of Ribā and Islamic Banking*, appeared to be difficult for some readers. In fact, a few eager students stated that they were able to understand the text only after they had read it two or three times. This book tries to simplify some of the difficult areas of juristic interpretation. Some additional explanations have been added as compared to our last attempt in 1995, in the book mentioned.

A major problem has been the recognition, by modern ulama and scholars, of some basic truths about the prohibition of *ribā*. This non-recognition sometimes appears to be a reluctance to face a few harsh realities and a tendency to evade thorny issues. One such issue is the prohibition of all loans, other than what we have come to call a charitable loan or *qard ḥasan*. The issue lies at the heart of all Islamic banking. Instead of giving arguments on this issue and responding to the arguments made in favour of such prohibition, our modern scholars and leading muftis maintain total silence. The present book includes at least one instance of such evasion. It is only when a response on this issue is available from modern schoars that knowledge in this area will advance further. Without such a discussion, Islamic banking has very little chance of success.

www.ingramcontent.com/pod-product-compliance
Lightning Source LLC
Chambersburg PA
CBHW070047210526
45170CB00012B/607
9781541245914